WAKE UP!

WAKE UP!

IT'S TIME TO SAY **YES** TO CREATING
A LIFE WORTH LOVING

JACKIE PFLUG

Published and distributed by Soul Speak Press.

Library of Congress Control Number: 2025900999
Pflug, Jackie
Wake Up! It's Time to Say Yes to Creating a Life Worth Loving

ISBN: 978-1-958472-29-3 (paperback)

ISBN: 978-1-958472-30-9 (eBook)

This work is nonfiction and, as such, reflects the author's memory of her experiences.

To my son Tanner.

You inspire me and lift me up.

I love you to the moon and back.

Surrender to what is,
let go of what was,
have faith in what will be.

—SONIA RICOTTI

CONTENTS

FOREWORD

You were drawn to this book because Jackie is a magnet. Jackie Pflug is a rare individual and I hope one day you will get to meet her or hear her speak. She has a warmth, wisdom, and charisma that makes others gravitate towards her. I first met Jackie when she attended one of my personal growth workshops in Tucson, Arizona. I clearly remember how expressive and open she was and how she freely offered support to the other attendees. She was the exact type of person I love having in my workshops . . . open, curious, and enthusiastic about learning. I have had the pleasure of working with Jackie over the past year and after reading this book. now I realize that how she showed up in my class that day was an authentic representation of her true character.

It takes a high level of self-reflection and emotional resilience to write a book like this. A book that talks about fear, suffering, and loss and turns it into lessons on strength, perseverance, and growth. I have often shared with Jackie that she impresses me with her "can do" attitude and now that I read this collection of remarkable stories, I am convinced that Jackie can do just about anything!

With a plethora of self-help information available nowadays, it is easy to fall into the trap of overconsumption and underutilization. What I mean by that is, it is easy to learn a lot about emotional wellness and personal growth, but not actually integrate the tools into our lives. Thankfully, that is *not* Jackie. She really is a personal growth warrior!

As you will see in this book, Jackie 1.0 was an adventurous and resilient woman. Somehow, Jackie has taken all of her past experiences, achievements, triumphs, challenges, and hardships and has evolved into the highest version of herself. I am proud to introduce the world to Jackie 2.0.

Love and light,
MICHELLE FRALEY, MA, WPCC

PREFACE

Darlin' do not fear what you don't really know
—BRETT DENNEN, "DARLIN' DO NOT FEAR"

I started thinking about writing my second book about seven years ago, but I wasn't sure what I would write about. Life got busy and I started living life on cruise control as a mom, daughter, and wife. I put the book idea on the back burner. During my weekly preventive maintenance appointment with my chiropractor Dr. Michael Isaacson, he said something that sparked memories of the summer of 1979 when my best friend Barb Wilson and I spent the summer at her parents' mountain cabin in Ruidoso, New Mexico. As I started telling him heartwarming and humorous stories about it, I was convinced my new book would be a compilation of stories from childhood to where I am today. I had found my inspiration.

As I began writing nonstop, what I didn't know was that something big was about to happen in my life—something really big. My life as I knew it was about to be turned upside down. Ready or not, I was about to tackle some incredibly difficult issues that I never

3

saw coming. But, like a phoenix rising from the ashes, I was about to go through a huge transformation, and I would emerge stronger, smarter, and more attuned to my Inner Voice than ever before.

The transformation that was about to happen would change everything about me. I got a second divorce. I dissolved dysfunctional relationships where I was spending time with people who were critical and didn't want the best for me. The music I listened to changed from '60s and '70s music to listening to artists like Michael Franti & Spearhead, P!nk, Jason Mraz, Bruno Mars, Andy Grammer, Train, Brett Dennen, Taylor Swift, and Jack Johnson. I sold my beautiful home and moved away from a neighborhood I loved. I changed the style of the clothes that I wore and the type of food that I ate. I changed the thoughts that came through me, how I loved, who I loved, what I spent my time on, how I showed up for the people around me, my values, the car that I drove—everything.

Transformations are opportunities to make changes in our lives. In the Hallmark movie *It Was Always You*, Elizabeth's engagement plans are thrown into disarray when her fiancé's brother David returns home. His unexpected influence prompts Elizabeth to question her life decisions. David tells her she is entitled to chase her own happiness. Elizabeth asks, "What will people think?" He responds by saying, "People around you aren't going to understand your journey and that's okay. They don't need to. It's not for them."

The book you are holding in your hands includes not only my collection of stories but also that two-year transformation and what I've learned from it. I like to look at my transformation as finding Jackie 2.0, much like the character Dory does in the movies *Finding Nemo* and *Finding Dory*.

Dory has a remarkable ability to overcome challenges, and her unwavering optimism and perseverance is encapsulated in her famous mantra "Just keep swimming." Dory's kindness, selflessness, and will-ingness to help Marlin find his son, despite just meeting him, show the power of friendship and living in the present moment. Dory's story ultimately teaches us about the importance of self-acceptance, the strength found in diversity, and the power of maintaining a positive attitude in the face of adversity.

Like Dory, I'm not afraid to share all the wonderful things I learned and the painful choices I had to make to get back to living an authentic, peaceful, happy, joyful, healthy life. Throughout the years, I had gotten so far away from myself that I didn't even recognize who I had become. I was making choices that weren't aligning with who I wanted to be so I wouldn't hurt other people's feelings, just to keep the peace and not rock the boat. In the end, it was too painful to continue a life without joy than to boldly make the necessary and difficult changes to grow and learn.

I had compromised what I wanted and what was important to me for way too long. My intuition was screaming for me to find a way out. Somewhere along the way, I heard someone say, "What's good for one person is good for the next," meaning the choices we make that affect others will eventually be good for them even though it may not be clear right away. That kept me going.

So many people who heard me speak during my career as a motivational speaker wanted to know what was next for me and what I was looking forward to after I retired. Well, this book is about what is next for me. At age sixty-nine, I'm certainly not at the end of my journey—in fact, my journey is just beginning. It's a journey that keeps evolving as I keep evolving.

What's keeping you stuck in a life you aren't satisfied with? I'm hoping my book will allow you the time to breathe and take time out of your day to really look at what you want in your life. Note that what I'll share with you is my pathway to a better life for me. Yours may look different. All it takes is a desire to change.

INTRODUCTION

On November 23, 1985, EgyptAir Flight 648, bound from Athens, Greece, to Cairo, Egypt, was hijacked and forced to land on the island of Malta. The hijackers, members of a dissident Palestinian faction, shot several passengers and threw them down the boarding ramp. The drama ended nearly twenty-four hours later when Egyptian commandos stormed the plane; of the ninety-eight passengers, thirty-eight people survived and sixty people died.

I was one of the thirty-eight survivors. At the time, I was a thirty-year-old special education teacher from Texas. After being shot in the head by a hijacker and left to die on the tarmac for five hours, my recovery process was challenging. I suffered epileptic seizures, severe depression, visual and hearing problems, short-term memory loss, and PTSD.

In my book *Miles to Go Before I Sleep: My Grateful Journey Back from the Hijacking of EgyptAir Flight 648*, I recount the hijacking in dramatic detail along with my physical and mental health struggles during my recovery. (Note that in 2011 (after 9/11) the book was rereleased

as *Miles to Go Before I Sleep: A Survivor's Story of Life After a Terrorist's Hijacking.*)

In a span of forty-eight hours, I had been kidnapped, held hostage, went through a hijacking, a gun battle in the air, and shot in the head point-blank. However, healing from those two days of terror took over thirty-five years and counting. After going through the first year of recovery, someone told me that what happened to me was so huge and horrible, how could anything else compare? Perhaps, because it was so big, I had gotten the big, bad thing out of the way at an early age and nothing from then on could compare. I was pretty sure that life didn't work that way, but as time went on, I bought into the idea. I learned quickly that was not the case at all.

What came after that hijacking wasn't easy. Three years after, I went through a divorce. In my second marriage, I experienced a miscarriage that shook me to my core. At age forty-eight, I was diagnosed with stage 3 colon cancer when I was a mom of a six-year-old. I've had five breaks on my right foot and four breaks on my left foot. Through all the hardships and challenges that came my way, I have to say I didn't handle them so graciously right away.

My grandma Nink once told me, "Good always comes from what appears to be bad." When I heard this at the age of twenty-nine, it didn't mean much to me. But once I survived the hijacking and head injury repercussions, I wondered, *How could something good come from this?* But, I immediately saw that goodness in the nurses, doctors, and other everyday "angels" that showed up in my recovery. My grandma showed me what it meant to be at peace through her attitude, words, actions, and calmness throughout each day. Regrettably, she died at age ninety-two, four months before the hijacking.

What enabled me to endure the impossible was something I refer to as my "Inner Voice." You know, it's that little voice in your head that sometimes pops up out of nowhere. It's like having a personal coach or a really smart friend living rent free in your brain. Sometimes it's a gut feeling, other times it's a random thought that just feels right. It's not always logical—it's more like a hunch or a feeling you can't shake. I often call it my God voice.

Some people think it's your subconscious piecing things together, while others believe it's something more spiritual. Everyone experiences it differently—maybe it's a whisper, a feeling in your stomach, or one of those lightbulb moments. Learning to tune into this inner GPS can be super helpful for making decisions or figuring out what you really want. My Inner Voice served me well during the hijacking as it prodded me to do something which ultimately saved my life.

HOW A SPLIT-SECOND DECISION DURING A HIJACKING CHANGED MY LIFE

During the hijacking, I had an experience while on the plane that made me think differently about the way I was living and thinking. The hijacking took place right after takeoff. Several hours into the flight, after experiencing a gun battle in the air between one security guard and three hijackers, I was sure that my life might be ending very soon. I was in shock, not only from the violent hijacking that was taking place in front of me, but because I always believed that I had so much time left on earth as I was only thirty.

I thought about my thirty years here on earth. While I did a few things that I was very proud of, there was a part of me that worried over the smallest things, didn't always tell the truth, gossiped, and got caught up wondering what others thought of me.

The hijackers took everyone's passports early into the hijacking. At about 4:00 a.m., after we made an emergency landing on the island of Malta, the hijackers came looking for the three Americans on board. Scarlett Rogenkamp, Patrick Baker, and myself. We were brought to the front of the aircraft. Patrick was in front of me, and Scarlett was behind me. There were three empty seats in the front row of the aircraft on my right facing the cockpit. They tied our hands behind our backs with neckties.

Patrick took the aisle seat. I got to choose whether to take the middle or window seat. With my hands tied behind me, I thought it would be easier to go around Patrick's knees and throw myself down on the middle seat. I was about to sit down, when my Inner Voice kicked in and said, "Take the window seat."

I argued with the thought as I was exhausted from lack of sleep and being in the middle of a terrorist hijacking; I didn't want to listen. As I resisted, the thought became stronger. As I passed by Patrick's long legs, I decided to take the window seat. Taking the window seat saved my life. I was still shot in the head, thrown from the plane, lost part of my vision, endured epilepsy, short-term memory loss, PTSD, and other symptoms related to trauma. But I lived.

Because of that experience with my Inner Voice, I began to hear and listen to the thoughts and ideas that were coming through me. Listening to my Inner Voice has kept me from doing things that weren't good for me and has made my life more fun and enjoyable. For that, I am grateful.

THE JEOPARDY! TUNE OF HEALING: FINDING JOY IN UNEXPECTED PLACES

At the age of fifty-seven, I fell down a flight of stairs and broke my ankle for the eighth time. My vision is limited from the gunshot wound, so there are times when I'm in a hurry, I miss a step or two going up or down stairs. This time it was my left ankle, and I noticed there was a scrape on my ankle from falling. I was put in a boot and given crutches.

The scrape became infected and red, and the pain was incredibly intense. My Inner Voice was telling me to take myself to the ER one particular night after my son's soccer game. Unfortunately, I chose to let someone change my mind that night. I went to bed in pain. I spent the week going in and out of doctor's offices looking for answers and help. By the end of the week I went to the ER and the orthopedic surgeon at the emergency room realized that I was in trouble. He said that the infection had become septic, and I was in danger of losing my right foot. *Losing my right foot?*

I woke up from surgery and my right foot was still intact. By not listening to my Inner Voice, I put myself in danger of losing my right foot. After the surgery, I found out that I had to take antibiotics twice a day for a minimum of thirty-two days. The septic poison was still in my system, and I needed strong antibiotics to fight it. I was told that because it was an extremely strong antibiotic, I needed a PICC line—a long, thin tube that's inserted through a vein in the arm and passed through to the larger veins near the heart. The antibiotic came in something that looked like a grenade.

After coming back from the hospital, my friend Dona Watson quickly offered to come to my house, once in the morning to connect the PICC line to the antibiotic grenade and then three hours later to disconnect it. Someone else helped with the evening dose.

Dona showed up two times a day, every day in the morning for thirty-two days no matter what. The first time she connected the antibiotic grenade to the PICC line coming out of my arm, she began to sing the Jeopardy! theme song. I looked at her and I began to laugh

11

so hard that I cried. She hummed that Jeopardy! song each time as she connected and disconnected the line. To this day, when I hear that song, I can see my sweet friend Dona with a smile on her face and her cute outfits that she wore while she told stories to keep my mind off the pain.

Angels come in all shapes and sizes. Having Dona by my side made the road to healing a lot easier.

CHAPTER ONE

RETURNING TO MALTA

A Journey of Gratitude and Healing

The day you can be grateful for every single trifle in your life, for the moving train, for the water that runs down a tap when you open it, for the light that comes on when you press a switch, for clean sheets on your bed . . . your heart will be filled with a deep contentment and with almost continuous joy. The key to being joyful is to always be grateful.

—ANTHONY DE MELLO, *SADHANA: A WAY TO GOD*

In November 1985, when I was leaving the Malta hospital to fly to Germany for my initial recovery after the hijacking, I wondered if I would ever recover and feel like myself again. As my husband Scott and I were taken to the Malta airport, I thought about how this little

island (seventeen miles long and nine miles wide) in southern Europe situated in the Mediterranean saved my life although I never got to see the beauty. I asked Scott, "What is Malta like?" Scott replied, "It is absolutely beautiful, and everyone here has been so nice."

That's when I said, "One day I'll come back to visit." I immediately wondered why I said that. I had no idea when or why I would come back to the island of Malta as this was where I experienced the most traumatic event of my life. But somehow, I knew that I would be back to visit.

Several years later, I was feeling a nudge that now might be a good time to make plans to go back to Malta. I didn't have the answers to why I needed to go as nothing seemed to make sense, I just knew I needed to go.

It was nearly twenty years since the hijacking took place, and my Inner Voice was telling me it was time to start planning the trip to go back to Malta where my life started over . . . but I had a busy life being a wife, mom, and my job as a speaker, how was I going to manage this trip? Yet, I knew two things: I was determined to go back, and I wanted to bring someone with me. I began to save money to pay for the ten-day trip for myself and a companion. Once I decided to make the trip, a series of events started to take place that seemed to come out of nowhere.

I had a list of people I wanted to ask to join me, but one by one, they said no. While I was planning my trip, I received an email from Pierre Calleja, the assistant police commissioner of Malta, asking if I would share any video clips that I might have that would be helpful from a hostage point of view that he could provide to his hostage negotiation team.

I told him that I was coming to Malta soon; he couldn't believe it. I told him there were four places that I wanted to visit. I wanted to go to the airport, hospital, the *Times of Malta* newspaper, and the police station. And finally, I wanted to meet the surgeon who operated on me and saved my life.

I asked him if he could help me get into those places. He said, "Yes, I can help you with all of that, and I can recommend a hotel for you to stay at that is close to every place you want to visit." I was amazed how everything seemed to be falling into place, but I still needed to pick a day to leave, book the airline tickets, and find someone to go with me.

In early December, I was having lunch with my business coach and best friend Mark LeBlanc at Murray's restaurant in downtown Minneapolis. Mark helped me grow my speaking business over the years and I leaned on him in times of struggle as well. We always met once a month for lunch, and today was a holiday lunch. Mark knew about my upcoming trip to Malta. I went on and on about how I just needed to find someone to go with me and how frustrating it was that everyone I asked said no. That's when I asked him if he would be open to going with me back to Malta.

I will never forget his response. He said, "I thought you would never ask." With tears rolling down my face, I said, "Really, you would go with me?" He said "Yes, of course I will be happy to carve out ten days to escort you there." I held onto his hand and said a heartfelt, "Thank you."

WHY MALTA? THE LIGHTBULB MOMENT

As we made plans, the reason why I needed to go back to Malta now was still gnawing at me. I just knew it was important to do so. I booked our flights and reserved two hotel rooms for ten nights. Everything was inked in our calendars. As the days went by, I was both excited and apprehensive. I had no idea what to expect.

I knew the bonus would be experiencing the beauty of Malta that Scott referred to. Three days before we were to leave, I was taking a shower and asking myself once again, "Why am I going to Malta?" The thought and answer suddenly came to me, "Thank you—you're going back to say thank you." It was crystal clear. I was going back to say thank you to people on the island for saving my life. It was my mission to find as many people as I possibly could who had saved my life twenty years before on November 24, 1985.

I was going back to Malta simply out of gratitude. I got out of the shower and quickly called Pierre Calleja and asked him if he could help me find people that were there that fateful day. He was happy to oblige. I started to pull together photos, articles, and items to share letting the people of Malta know I had recovered and was leading a good life because of them. It was overwhelming pulling everything together and I was thankful to God for the wonder of it all. It was a miracle how everything was coming together. I was so excited to be a part of it. Without Pierre, we would have had no one to guide us to our destinations. Pierre was my angel in disguise. He made all things possible. With him and Mark by my side, I was in good hands.

BIRTHDAY FLIGHTS AND HEARTFELT REUNIONS

Finally, the day of our trip arrived. It was January 24, 2006, Mark and I were at the Minneapolis-Saint Paul International Airport. It also happened to be my fifty-first birthday. As we walked to our gate, Mark asked the gate agent a few questions.

He came back, sat down, and surprised me with two first-class upgrades so we could be more comfortable on our way. He later shared he had no idea if he had enough airline miles, but he thought there was no harm in asking. It is still one of the best birthday presents I have ever received.

After a long night and two flights, we landed at the airport in Valletta, the capital of Malta. We took a taxi to the hotel and checked in. I was exhausted and ready to sleep, but excited to begin this journey into the unknown. I was nervous, too, about the enormity of it all, but was happy I had Mark at my side.

Our first day in Malta, we visited the hospital. The hospital looked like it was from the 1940s, and we had gone back in time. I felt honored that I was able to meet many of the doctors and nurses who were an integral part of the story I never knew.

They were surprised to see me and were filled with emotion. They shared vivid memories of that day. They showed me the room where I stayed as well as the Intensive Care Unit. One of the nurses told me that when the ambulance brought me in, I was fighting with them with my arms, trying to get loose, thinking they were the hijackers.

As I stood by them, listening to their story of how that day affected each of them, my heart was filled with heartache and gratitude. I took out my photos to show them what kind of life I went on to lead because they saved me. I gave them each a hug and thanked them for being there for me that day and saving my life.

As we were leaving the hospital, Pierre shared with us that in five days, the hospital was being demolished and a new hospital would be constructed. I couldn't believe what I was hearing. I realized that the timing of our trip became even more profound—now I knew why my Inner Voice was so persistent about the timing of our trip.

Later that day, I was lucky to have lunch with Dr. Zrinzo, who operated on me following the shooting. He told me the coolness of the day and the light rain saved my life. It protected me as I laid on the tarmac for five hours before I was taken to the hospital. He also told me that he made the decision to wait to operate on my brain as he did not believe my body could handle the operation when I first came in. I gave him a big hug and thanked him for saving my life. I realized that so many people had a hand in watching over me and taking care of me.

RETRACING STEPS: FROM POLICE ARCHIVES TO THE TARMAC OF REFLECTION

Pierre had been in charge of our itinerary, and I never said no to any of his suggestions. My response was a strong affirmative "yes!"

The next day we went to the police station. I met the police officers and as we chatted, Pierre gave Mark access to the archives, evidence, and news clippings and photographs that were filed away. I decided to pass on seeing that part of my past.

Mark never shared with me what he saw, read, or what Pierre told him about that tragic day, but I know that visit to the police station deeply impacted him.

As we made our way to the airport, we met the director of security. We were given complete access to the airport and a tour of what actually goes on behind the curtains that very few people see or even know about. With the director of security driving, we made our way to what seemed to be a very far distance from the airport, away from the beaten path. We were taken to a special part of the airport where if a hijacking or other catastrophic event occurs, the plane is taxied away from the airport, seemingly out in the middle of nowhere. Now I knew why it seemed like no one was around, no city lights, no lights from the airport, no one. That was always a mystery to me, almost as if we had been abandoned and on our own during the hijacking.

Nothing could be further from the truth. As we got out of the car, I asked the director where he thought the plane was parked that day. I imagined the nose of the plane in the area he told me, I walked a few steps to where I thought the cockpit was and then a few more steps to where I might have been sitting on the aisle bulkhead seat that day in 1985. As the director, Mark, and Pierre were talking quietly among themselves away from me, I sat down on the tarmac cross-legged, bowed my head, and closed my eyes. I thought about Patrick and Scarlett and all the people who had been on that flight and had either lost their lives or had somehow survived on that tragic day.

I thought about my mom and dad, friends, and former husband Scott. I thought about Tanner, my nine-year-old son, and all the lives that were forever impacted by three terrorists. I whispered a prayer of thanksgiving. I thanked God for all the blessings I have received and for this incredible experience of coming back to Malta. I got up from the tarmac, wiped the tears from my eyes, and walked over to Mark.

AN UNEXPECTED ENCOUNTER: HEALING A HIDDEN HERO

As we got into the car to drive back to the airport, the director asked if we wanted to go to the airport control tower. I looked at Mark and we both said yes. As I was standing in the middle of the control tower looking out at the Malta airport runway where negotiations took place many years ago, it was not lost on me how fortunate I was to be alive and in Malta

We eventually made our way back to the main airport terminal via a building where the administrative offices were located. As we walked through the hallway, there seemed to be loud conversation coming from one of the offices.

A supervisor appeared in the hallway and stopped us. She informed me that there was someone who wanted to meet me if he could. I agreed and we were taken into the office where there were several people working in cubicles.

When a man came up to me with tears in his eyes, I had a feeling he might have been at the airport that day of the hijacking. He told me he was near me as I was lying on the tarmac. In fact, he was so close, he could see me fading in and out of consciousness.

He was a member of a sniper team that was similar to the SWAT team that we have in the United States. Little did I know, this team was all around me camouflaged in hiding, waiting for orders to engage the terrorists. As he shared his story, I could feel him shaking as he was overcome with emotion. The experience of being so close and yet unable to come to my aid had devastated him. In fact, so much so, he resigned his position from the military shortly after the hijacking. He took an administrative position at the airport and for many years, he had been consumed with guilt and grief. I wrapped my arms around him, and we cried together.

I told him he helped save my life and I went on to have a good life with a family and a son. I showed him pictures and I assured him how grateful I was for him and especially now knowing I was never alone on that tarmac.

FROM PRESS CONFERENCES TO 'CRAZY BINGO'

Later that night, we met Pierre's mother, his girlfriend, and sister at his mom's house for dinner. They even tried to set up Mark with Pierre's sister. The food was amazing, and the conversation was a much-needed reprieve from a hard day.

The next day, Pierre wanted to set up a press conference. I agreed. It only lasted for about an hour, but it was hard. Afterwards, I was able to meet so many people behind the scenes. When I was done, I noticed in the back of the room two tall burly men in brown leather jackets looking at me. I walked over to them and asked if they were there that day of the hijacking. They said yes. I asked them what their jobs were. They told me they were the ones who took all the dead bodies off the airplane and took them to the morgue.

They appeared to be around my age, so they would have been about thirty years old when they had those jobs. I told them I was so sorry that they had to go through that and thanked them for what they did. We talked a little longer and then hugged each other as we said goodbye. As they turned around, I heard one of them whisper to the other man, "No one has ever thanked us before." I turned away and looked for a chair to sit down on and began to cry.

I didn't realize the enormity and the trickle-down effects of the hijacking on the island. Pierre told me that the US ambassador to Malta wanted to meet and asked if I had time to visit. I jumped at the chance to do so. I met the young ambassador at her home where I soon discovered she was a young mom as there was a crib and bouncy chair within arm's length. She thanked me for coming and told me she read a lot about the hijacking. During our heartfelt conversation she said something that stuck with me and truly propelled my motivational speaking career. She said, "It's important not to forget history." That's when I realized why it was so important to me to have a speaking career—to tell my story and the lessons learned and to keep that part of history alive.

One evening, while walking back to the hotel after dinner, we saw a sign for bingo. It was over, but the next night and the four nights following that, Mark and I played bingo. Bingo in Malta was not like the slow letter and number calling I was used to back in the United States. In Malta, they rattle off the letters and numbers so fast, it's almost impossible to keep up. We referred to it as "Crazy Bingo." It made me laugh. We went back each night as it was a good way to let go of our emotions from the day. It was a welcome distraction from the heaviness of the trip.

As our plane landed in Minneapolis, I couldn't wait to hold my little boy Tanner. All I could think about was how this amazing trip came out of a single thought, *I'm going back to Malta one day.* And that's what I did. An added bonus was it was the twentieth anniversary of the hijacking and my birthday. It just goes to show that when you put a single thought out there into the air, you never know how it will turn out. Planning and during the trip I never felt scared. Instead, I felt more feelings of wonderment, excitement, and, of course, sadness. On the drive home, I thought to myself, *I am so lucky!* I felt lucky that the trip turned out so well and that we were safe. In my heart, I always knew we'd be safe. I felt so grateful for Pierre and his willingness to be our escort. It was pure serendipity.

MARK'S PERSPECTIVE: EMOTIONAL ENCOUNTERS AND PIVOTAL MOMENTS IN MALTA

I wanted a fresh perspective from my travel companion Mark about the trip. He experienced it through very different eyes than me as he was there to support me. Since we are such good friends, I thought it would be best if my book editor interviewed him. She did so and the following are excerpts from their interview.

We stepped into this world and neither of us knew what to expect. Pierre was incredibly gracious and just a wonderful man. Right away we recognized we were on an adventure and Pierre was at the helm. He was happy to be our guide as Jackie is somewhat of a celebrity in Malta as she survived the biggest tragic event ever to happen in Malta.

A trip highlight for me was when Pierre took us to the police station where he retrieved bankers boxes of evidence and photographs. While Jackie chose not to go into the evidence room, I was open to it. I began looking through pages of photos. These detectives photographed everything—every bullet on the ground, and each body that had burned in the explosion. I felt like I had a front row seat into a moment in history that really changed the world.

Think about it, in 1985, there were no real international laws regarding safety measures in airports when it came to passenger safety. No matter where you lived, you didn't need to go through security to reach the airport gate. The Transportation Security Administration (TSA) was established by the Aviation and Transportation Security Act, which was signed into law by President George W. Bush on November 19, 2001. The TSA was created in response to the terrorist attacks on September 11, 2001, which killed nearly three thousand people.

So many lives were lost in the hijacking of EgyptAir Flight 648. Even today, airport security around the world is using that hijacking experience as a training module because so many mistakes were made. As I was going through the photographs, Pierre shared some things with me about inherent errors in the negotiation tactics because of who the negotiator was.

We got to go up into the tower where these negotiations were being handled. These are things that ordinary people don't get to do, so this was the experience of a lifetime. However, the most significant moment of the entire experience was when we were at the location where the plane was parked. Believe it or not, every airport has a designated hijacking area. Know that if there is something that happens in the air and there's a landing and there's a problem that there is a place where the airplane is taxied to so it's away from the terminals. It's by itself.

That's one of the reasons why Jackie thought during the hijacking that they landed in a desert, not an actual airport. There were no buildings. They couldn't see anything out the window. So they were really confused. They just landed at an airport and there were no trucks, no baggage people, and no terminal that they could see out the window. They were alone in a desolate area of the airport.

For me, the most memorable extraordinary moment of the trip, or even maybe my life, was when Jackie met the man from the sniper team. We couldn't figure out why he was crying. It turns out he worked in the offices at the airport now, but he was there the day of the hijacking. In fact, he was on the sniper team. I don't know how many feet away, but he was in camouflage gear. He was just waiting for the moment that they could shoot one of the terrorists. This particular gentleman who was young in his career was out on the tarmac when Jackie was thrown onto it.

He could see she was alive, yet he couldn't do anything about it as he was given a directive that he couldn't help her. So, he lay on the ground, camouflaged for five hours watching her breathe. It destroyed him and it's why he left the secret forces and got an office job at the airport. It haunted him to this day that he was never able to help her in her time of need. And, of course, they never expected her to live. It was incredibly emotional meeting Jackie as he probably never thought in a million years he would see her again. He got a chance to apologize to her for not coming to her aid, which was what he had wanted to do for twenty years. It had haunted him every day of his life that he was not able to help her in that tragedy.

Jackie listened to him and hugged him saying it was okay. I just couldn't get over it—that we were able to meet this man simply by chance. Everything had to be perfect for us to be walking down that hallway as he stepped forward. It was a moment meant to be right. And it was just so incredibly powerful and gripping.

Moments like these were why we needed the downtime each night. Like clockwork, around 4:00 p.m. we'd get back to the hotel, take a nap, play bingo, and then get something to eat. The first night we saw the bingo sign, it was after dinner and we vowed we would give it a try. At night, we'd walk by beautiful fountains and spontaneously go to different restaurants. We never had a reservation as we wanted our evenings to be more relaxed and not as structured as our day's itinerary.

Of course, meeting the surgeon that saved her life was amazing. He told her the cool, rainy weather aided her recovery instead of it being 90 degrees and sunny. The nurses recalled Jackie shouting, "You're going to shave my head? You're going to cut my jeans off? Don't shave my head and don't cut my jeans off!" I know it felt good for everyone to have a good laugh and release some of the heavy emotions of the trip.

It was the trip of a lifetime and I'm so glad I was able to share it with my good friend Jackie. She is my role model when it comes to saying yes to new experiences. She has shown me how being open to new experiences can create a whole new world. This trip opened up that world to me and made me realize how precious life is. Jackie going to Malta to thank these people was not only cathartic for her, but also for them.

TRUSTING THE JOURNEY: MY INNER VOICE LED ME TO MALTA

This trip to Malta was something I had planned all along, but I didn't know when it would be the right time. Something amazing happened when I gave away the timeline to my Higher Power or Inner Voice. When I listened to the plan, I made it happen. I'm so grateful I did. It transformed my life and being able to experience it with my best friend was something I'll never regret.

I'm so happy Mark said yes to my invitation without skipping a beat!

THE ART OF LETTING GO: HONORING OUR POSSESSIONS WITH GRATITUDE

Just like my trip to Malta was all about saying thank you to the people that saved my life, I also have an attitude of gratitude when it comes to my possessions. There's something about appreciating what I have and knowing when it's time to let some of my possessions go. I actually talk to my possessions and let them know that I've appreciated all the time that we've spent together. This is part of my process of letting go.

We can become attached to material possessions. So, for me it's important to recognize that. Whether it's my car, clothes, or even my computer or cell phone, when it's time to let something go, I say, "Thank you! I appreciate what you've done for me." I sold my convertible because I knew it was time to let it go. At the time, I had two cars, and I knew I had to choose between the two. Selling the convertible was the logical choice because you can't get through winter in Minnesota in a convertible. I told the car, "I appreciate you taking care of me, but it's time to let you go." I initially bought the convertible because I wanted to spend more time outside. That car allowed me to do that.

When my son got his driver's license, I gave him my old Subaru. A few years later, he got in an accident, and I encouraged him to have a conversation with the car. I said, "Let your car know that it's hurt and that you're going to take care of it. Let it know you're going to bring it somewhere to fix it up so you can drive it again. Apologize to the car for not being present."

He went outside and talked to the car like I requested even though he thought I was a little crazy and wasn't convinced that it would make a difference. And that was that. I wanted my son to know that things come into our lives, whether they're human beings or innate objects that help us get around and make our life easier. We need to be present with them.

I've noticed how an attitude of gratitude can provide a wide range of benefits that positively impact mental, physical, and emotional well-being. I've seen firsthand how gratitude fosters better relationships, increases empathy, and leads to greater life satisfaction and happiness. I embrace my attitude of gratitude and am forever grateful to the people of Malta and am so happy I took the initiative to revisit Malta on my fifty-first birthday.

CHAPTER 2

DARE TO AGREE

The Unexpected Joys of Saying Yes

Do something every day that scares you.
—ELEANOR ROOSEVELT

A magazine cover headline caught my eye one morning. It read, "Fear Less, Live More." It made me wonder if I was doing exactly that. I've always been a "yes" person since I was a young girl. If someone asked me to go somewhere or do something, for the most part, I said, "Yes." Saying yes to adventures and opportunities has served me well throughout my life. By saying Yes, I believe that I am able to fear less and live more.

TWO FRIENDS, ONE VAN: OUR EUROPEAN ADVENTURE

When I was in my early forties, my friend Debbie Reno asked me if I would travel with her to Europe. She wanted to see different countries, along with visiting her friend Ronnie, who was working for Exxon and living in Brussels, Belgium. I enthusiastically said, "Yes!" I suggested we travel through Europe in a VW camper van. It was something my former husband Scott and I had done many years before. I thought it was a great way to see Europe as we visited different campsites every night and cooked meals inside the van.

Debbie and I decided that I would be the driver, and she would be the navigator on our trip. We flew into Frankfurt, Germany, and took a taxi to the car rental place. As we listened to the young man go over the dos and don'ts of driving the VW camper van with us, I started to feel overwhelmed. Even though I had taken this trip before, this time I was the driver instead of Scott. I was the one in charge of getting us to and from our destinations safely.

We stopped at the restroom before we took off where both of us confided in each other that we were nervous. I jokingly said, "Let's just stay in this bathroom for ten days and tell everybody we had a great trip!" We laughed. We got into our newly rented VW camper van and off we went heading to the streets of Germany, France, Italy, the Netherlands, and Belgium. Debbie was well prepared with travel books and many maps of the locations we were planning to visit. Keep in mind, there were no cell phones or GPS in those days and traveling required a good navigator. As the days went on, we got comfortable in our roles as driver and navigator. We enjoyed the different camp-sites that we stayed at and the people we met along the way.

While in a small town in France, we were looking for a place to park our van so we could walk around and enjoy the scenery. After making a wrong turn, I decided to turn around in an apartment complex parking lot. I turned too quickly, and my back bumper got hooked onto the front bumper of a small car. We were stuck and couldn't move. We got out of the car to see what exactly had happened. We decided our best course of action was to go back and forth to try to unhook the cars.

I got back into the van while Debbie directed me on what to do. After ten minutes of going back and forth with the small car's bumper attached to my van, I was exhausted. I got out of the van and as I was trying to figure out what might be our next option, I took a deep breath and looked up. That's when I noticed the four-story apartment building with shared balconies on each floor. There were about fifteen young men in their twenties curiously watching Debbie and I as we tried to unhook the two cars.

I smiled up at them and waved. Even though they were on different balconies, almost in unison, they all waved back. I turned back to Debbie to determine our next move. What happened next was incredible. Each of those fifteen young men came down to help us. They took over our precarious situation. Some of them were speaking French while others were speaking English so Debbie and I could understand what they were saying.

They instructed me to get back into the van and go back and forth again while turning my wheel. No luck. They determined that the only way to unhook the vehicles was to lift up the smaller car and move it over. I told them that I didn't think that was a good idea. Before I knew it, they had lifted the car up and moved it over to the side. In an instant we were unhooked. I was jumping with joy! Debbie and I hugged each of the fifteen young men and told them we were so grateful they were there for us. We drove away and marveled how these men came out of nowhere to help us out of our predicament.

As we continued our trip through France, Debbie wanted to spend a day at Disneyland Paris, so we did. While waiting in line for one of the rides, a woman ahead of me was speaking a language I thought I recognized. I asked her where she was from. She said she was from Malta. She asked me if I had been there before. I said that I had. Although I didn't tell her my connection to Malta, I thought that meeting the woman was an amazing gift.

As it started to get dark, we headed back on the road to find a campsite to stay at for the night. As I became quite tired, I suggested that we stop at a hotel on the side of the road. At 2:00 a.m., as we approached the hotel's front door, we noticed there were many men walking around. After getting our keys, we walked to our room and went inside. The door didn't lock from the inside! Since things didn't feel quite right, something was telling me this was unsafe, and we needed to leave.

As we continued our drive, I realized I couldn't keep driving as I didn't have any energy left. We saw a rest stop for truckers. We agreed we would stay there and park our van. We locked the doors, closed the curtains on the windows, said a prayer for safety, and went to sleep. We got up the next morning, ate breakfast at the diner next to the truck stop, and visited with the truck drivers. After we left, we came upon the Autobahn, a network of freeways that connects major German cities. It's known for its high speeds as cars travel over 100 miles per hour and it's legal.

Getting on the Autobahn was a challenge with the slow-going camper van, but our first time getting on, we managed to pick up our speed to go with the traffic. I never heard so many horns honking at me to hurry up. We finally felt like we were part of the fast-paced group going down the Autobahn when we came upon a toll booth. We pulled over. As I opened my driver's car door to put the money in the toll booth, my purse dropped and spilled all over the road. I quickly scooped up my coins, cash, coin purse, and a pair of glasses. I didn't see anything else. I put everything in my purse, closed the door, and kept going.

We slowly got back onto the Autobahn and prayed that no one would hit us. As we picked up our speed, we were traveling about 80 miles per hour to keep up with the other cars. That's when a car with a family inside on my left began honking their horn and holding up my Clinique red lipstick that they had found when they went through the toll behind us. I rolled down my window and yelled out the window for them to keep it as we were going too fast. I knew that if I pulled over to get my lipstick, it would be dangerous for both cars to be on the side of the road.

They must not have heard me because they sped up, got in front of me, slowed down, and pulled over. I pulled up behind them. The woman got out of the car and ran back towards us. I opened up my car door, hoping no one would run us over as they were flying past us. The woman was lovely and didn't seem to be phased by the speeding cars. She gave me my lipstick and ran back to her car. I put my lipstick back in my purse, and away we went. That's life on the Autobahn!

When we returned to Houston after spending ten days on our Europe adventure, Debbie and I were grateful for all the memories we had made and the crazy stories we could share as a result of our trip.

EMBRACING THE UNEXPECTED AS A HOST FAMILY

When Tanner was a freshman in high school, I had been thinking about bringing an exchange student into our home, but I only knew of exchange students staying for a year, and I thought that might not be a good fit, so I let that idea go. Then, in May, I got an email from a Chinese teacher, Ergan Xu, from Eden Prairie High School. In July, forty-eight Chinese exchange students were coming to visit Eden Prairie, Minnesota, from their sister city Loudi, China. She was looking for host families for ten days. I knew that this was a great opportunity and very doable to host two exchange students for ten days instead of a year.

It turns out that every other year, they visit each other's city to connect and learn about each other's cultures in a way that can only be done by becoming completely immersed in a new world. That summer, Eden Prairie hosted the Chinese students and four adults. For many students, it would be their first time in America.

I checked in with my family to ask if this was something they might be interested in. Everybody said yes, so I let Ergan know that we'd like to be a host family. Since we had only one extra bedroom, I opted for two boys who could share the room. I was excited for Tanner to experience being with the boys as all the kids in the host families were allowed to join these kids on their daily activities of exploring Minneapolis and Saint Paul. We were assigned two boys, Jeff and Lucky. They were here to practice their English and learn about American culture. When they arrived, all the host families showed up at the airport, anxiously waiting for the exchange students they would be housing. We were there excitedly waiting too, even though we didn't really know much about the boys.

We introduced ourselves, welcomed them to Minnesota, got their luggage, and then took the boys to the parking ramp to get into the car. The three boys got in the back seat. As I looked behind me from the front seat, I noticed the two boys weren't wearing their seat belts. They had no idea what a seat belt was. We buckled them in and drove off to our home. Jeff and Lucky brought me gifts from their mothers which were so very sweet. One was a red tea set, a beautiful fan, and other trinkets from China. It was a way for the mothers to say thank you to me for watching over their boys.

As a host family, we were supposed to make meals as American style as possible. But I knew the boys might appreciate some Chinese food, so I went to an Asian grocery store and bought some dumplings for them. And they just went crazy for that. One night we took them to a Chinese restaurant, and they stuffed themselves because they really missed their food.

The next evening, we were just hanging out upstairs. The boys asked if Tanner and I wanted to see where they lived pointing to the computer. Tanner found a map and put in their address so we could see where they lived. They lived in a large apartment complex. It reminded me of a tour I took in San Francisco's Chinatown years before. There were a lot of benches, play equipment, and even a couch in the outside space. The tour guide explained that the outdoor space was essentially their living room. Their apartments are so small that they use the outdoor space to socialize.

Ergan wanted to have an American-outside get together for all the kids and their host families at the end of their stay. I offered to have a picnic and pool party at my home since we had a pool in our backyard. They had a budget for the food and anything else necessary to have a great party. That's when I asked how many people to expect. She responded, "About one hundred!!" I have this tendency to say yes and then figure out how to make it work. So, that's what I did. I started to go about planning the menu. Ergan requested American food. Immediately, I thought that Costco hot dogs are about as American as you can get. I would whip up some beans, buy some chips, and make some lemonade. She thought that sounded good. We'd also ask all the host families to contribute a dish to pass. We borrowed games that could be played outside like badminton, foosball, and beanbags. We put all those games in the front yard.

For safety due to the party size, I hired two female lifeguards from Eden Prairie High School, and when two of my friends heard me talking about the party, they volunteered to help. Renee offered to go to Costco to pick up the hot dogs. As she was standing in line in Costco, a woman behind her said she'd like to buy her dinner. She said, "It's on me today." Renee responded, "Oh, that's so nice of you, but I don't think you want to buy what I'm here to pick up—120 hot dogs!" The woman agreed that she wasn't up to buying 120 hot dogs.

The day unfolded like magic. I was so grateful that I could be a part of something like this. The weather was perfect, and the party lasted about four hours. For the first few hours everybody hung out in the front yard playing all the games. I went into the backyard to check on the two lifeguards. I started to laugh as nobody was in the pool for them to watch. We were wondering if anybody was going to go swimming.

After everyone ate, the kids started to get into the pool even though many of these kids had never swum before. I borrowed some extra life jackets. There were bumper-to-bumper kids in the shallow end of the pool. Those that wanted to give the deep end a try, put on a life jacket to see how that would feel for them. They were laughing and giggling and having the time of their lives. During the party, I stood on the deck watching the kids, thinking how the idea of wanting to be a host family turned into this beautiful thing that happened. It felt so good.

The day before they went back to China, all the kids and host families met at the Eden Prairie Courthouse for a final dinner together. The next day, we took the boys to the airport. All the host families were crying and saying goodbye to the kids. We knew we probably would never see them again. It was emotional. We got to experience what it was like to be a host family all in the span of ten days. The experience was something Tanner and I will never forget.

CHAPTER 3

ADVENTURES IN SAYING YES

Four Stories of Unexpected Journeys

A pessimist sees the difficulty in every opportunity;
an optimist sees the opportunity in every difficulty.
—WINSTON CHURCHILL

OOPS, I BOOKED AN EXTREME RAFTING TRIP: MY ACCIDENTAL OUTWARD BOUND ADVENTURE

I've always wanted to go on a white water rafting trip. When I was thirty-eight, I looked into a group called Outward Bound. I didn't know anything about white water rafting nor about Outward Bound. I had been white water canoeing in Texas in college years before. The

rapids on the Guadalupe River had been intense, so I felt like I had some experience and was comfortable to sign up for the ten-day rafting trip with Outward Bound. The trip started in Utah on the Green River, and we would make our way rafting into Colorado. I flew into Utah. So far, there were no red flags that warned me that perhaps this was not the rafting trip for me. I was so excited to learn how to white water raft. I wondered where we were going to sleep, what we were going to eat, and where we were going to go to the bathroom.

If Google had been around in the late '80s, I would have discovered that Outward Bound trips were more intense than I was ready or equipped for.

When I arrived at our meeting place in Utah, I soon discovered that we would be sleeping in one-man tents that we had to put together in the evening on our own and break down in the morning. We slept in our own sleeping bag that we brought with us, and we were to wake up when it was light outside, which was at 5:30 a.m.

The Outward Bound leaders brought the food ingredients for three meals a day, snacks, water, and rafts. Whatever we brought into the place where we camped, we had to bring out with us, even our poop! We were divided into three groups. One group made dinner, another cleaned up after dinner, and another group designed and put together a make-shift bathroom. We saw no one at all for ten days as we were the only ones on the river. We ate breakfast and lunch when we stopped at an opening to rest. Mountains were to our left and to our right.

I had never worked harder physically for something as I did with the trip. At night around 9:00 p.m. when everything was cleaned from dinner, we would gather around a fire built by one of the leaders and talk for an hour about the day and what we learned. All I wanted to do was go to sleep. Rafting was wonderful, everything else was hard—even talking.

The aches and pains I had in almost every one of my joints and muscles made it difficult to sleep in my little tent. Of all the adventures I said *yes* to, I was sure this was not going to be one of my favorites. *What was I thinking? Why did I not take the time to find out what Outward Bound was all about?* I wanted to go home, but I was stuck. We were in the middle of nowhere and the leaders warned us to be very careful in everything we did so as not to get injured or hurt because the only way out was on a helicopter, and it would take several hours to find help. *What was I thinking?*

On the rafting trip, I was extremely over my head in athletic ability that was needed to be on this trip. I looked at the other women and men and I could tell they had put in a lot of time and effort into being fit. Our ages ranged from twenty to forty years old. There were fifteen of us plus staff. On the third day, I noticed one of the women my age was crying. Oh, how I wanted to cry all day. I kept my crying to a minimum late at night while in my sleeping bag in my little tent. The staff visited with the woman, and she continued with the trip.

I had a conversation with her later that day. She told me that this was the hardest thing she had ever done, and she wanted to go home. I told her I felt the same. Since quitting was not an available option, I decided to start looking at the good around me. I loved seeing the bright stars at night, the bonfire, what I was learning about rafting and learning about how to be in the wilderness.

By the tenth day, I was becoming really good at rafting, and I felt an excitement that I had actually made it through an Outward Bound trip. It was a huge accomplishment. After I got home safely, some of my friends asked where I was. I told them I went white water rafting with a group called Outward Bound. "You did what?" they asked. One of them said, "Oh my goodness, why would you do that? You survived? That must have been so difficult!" And of course it was.

My friends knew Outward Bound was a nonprofit educational organization that serves people of all ages and backgrounds through challenging learning expeditions that inspire strength of character, leadership, and service to others, both in and out of the classroom. That information might have been helpful; however, it didn't matter.

Looking back, saying *yes* to Outward Bound gave me an experience that I will never forget. It helped me realize that I am stronger than I think I am and that I can see the good in even the hardest of things. For that, I am grateful.

Sometimes, saying *yes* and being open to new possibilities can build character. That reminds me of a story from my childhood when I was quick to say an enthusiastic *yes* while my coworkers chose to say *no*.

CLIMBING TANKERS AND MAKING FRIENDS: HOW I STRUCK GOLD WITH A CONVENIENCE STORE GIG

In 1972, when I was seventeen, I took a part-time job as a checkout clerk at Rice Food Market in Pasadena, Texas. When I was in high school, I worked there after school a few days a week. I also worked there during my freshman year at San Jacinto College. When I was a sophomore, I transferred to Sam Houston State University in Huntsville, Texas, and ultimately graduated in 1977. During the summer from my sophomore year to senior year, I moved back home to Pasadena, Texas, with my parents for three summers in a row. I knew I needed a summer job. I had experience running a cash register, so I applied at a convenience store like a 7-Eleven called Sellers Brothers.

The owner Gary Sellers hired me. I told him I could only work for three months during the summer, but I would show up every day and be on time. Somehow, each summer Gary Sellers had an opening for me to work.

For the next three years, I worked during June, July, and August, and then would go back to college each September. It didn't take me long to figure out that I hit the jackpot when it came to seasonal work. The other workers were such great people, and we had so much fun. Gary checked in on us occasionally, but the store pretty much worked like a family. Even the customers that came in on a regular basis felt like family. If it wasn't raining, I rode my bicycle to work as it was only a mile or two from my parents' house. After my shift, I always bought a 3 Musketeers bar, got on my bike, and headed home. Most days, I worked with Debbie. We were a good team.

The final summer I worked there, the Sellers Brothers had added gasoline to their convenience stores throughout town. It brought more customers into the store. Every time a gasoline tanker truck pulled in to deliver gasoline for the pumps, I got excited. Because computers weren't around just yet, before the driver could empty the gasoline into the tubs underground, someone from the store had to climb up on the ladder on the back of the gasoline truck, crawl on top of the tank to make sure each one of the five tubs in the truck was full of gasoline. There were about four or five lids to open and close on top of the tank in order to check for the gasoline, and then we had to crawl back down off the tanker. Once the gasoline was emptied into the tubs below ground, someone from the store had to go back up to the top of the tank, crawl to each lid, open it to make sure the gasoline was all gone, close the lids, and crawl back down.

I loved doing that job! I always volunteered. One day, one of my male coworkers wanted to give it a try. Once he finished, he said, "I'm never doing that again!" I always wondered who did that job after I left to become a teacher. Many years later, there were computers and climbing on top of gasoline tankers was a thing of the past. Today, as I tell that story now and again, I often wonder if people even believe me. What fun I had working at Sellers Brothers in Pasadena, Texas!

THE ONE-NIGHT COCKTAIL WAITRESS: A LESSON IN KNOWING WHEN TO QUIT

In the summer of 1979 when I was twenty-five, my best friend Barb and I stayed in her parents' cabin in the mountains of Ruidoso, New Mexico. At the time, we were both elementary education teachers and had the summers off. I was in my third year of taking part-time summer classes at the University of Houston-Clear Lake City to earn my master's degree in education. I was exhausted and needed a break. We lived in their cabin during the months of June, July, and August of that year. It seemed like a fun adventure, and I was excited to see where it would lead us.

We knew we wanted to work and make some extra money. Barb saw an ad in the Ruidoso newspaper. A new country-western dance hall was looking for cocktail waitresses. We both wanted to give it a try as we had never done anything like this before. Neither of us had any experience whatsoever as a waitress, but they hired us anyway. They gave us a list of drinks and we had to memorize the garnishes that went with them. Barb and I were both terribly inexperienced when it came to alcoholic drinks. At age twenty-three, I had my first alcoholic drink—a beer. I was very naïve. Before starting, we both stayed up late two nights in a row memorizing what garnishes went with what drinks.

Finally, it was the dance hall grand opening. We had to be there at 3:00 p.m. and the doors were to open at 5:00 p.m. It took me all but five minutes once people started to arrive to realize that I was in way over my head. I kept mixing up everyone's drinks and I was constantly putting the wrong garnishes on them. I had never heard of any of the drinks that people were ordering. I was frustrated and overwhelmed. No matter how hard I tried, I just couldn't keep up. The owner told us not to sit down or take a break until the bar closed.

At one point, my feet were so tired—I felt like the only way to sit down was to go to the bathroom. I went into a stall, locked the door, and took my feet off the floor to hide so no one would know I was sitting down. I was sure it was midnight, and we only had two more hours left to work. I looked at my watch—it was only 8:00 p.m. and we had six more hours to work I couldn't believe it! Tears streamed down my face, and I felt defeated. Then, I heard someone in the bathroom whispering loudly, "Jackie, are you in here?" It was Barb. I whimpered, "Yes, I'm here. This is so hard."

That's when she told me that she just tipped over a pink colored drink on a woman's white pants. I laughed. I told her that this job was not a good fit for me and that I was going to quit in the morning. After we got back home to the cabin late that night, Barb tried to talk me out of quitting and to just try it one more night. I got up the next morning and called our boss. I said, "I am so sorry, but I need to quit." I looked at Barb and gave the phone to her. She told him that she quit too. Our boss was not happy. I was confident that we would find work that was a better fit where we could laugh, have fun, and meet interesting people, and I trusted that our boss would find someone who was better suited for the job.

A few days later, we were hired at Ruidoso Downs Race Track as tellers. We met the most amazing jockeys and trainers and were able to work with people we liked and be in a job that made sense for us. Looking back, it probably was a precursor to being open to having equine therapy. To this day, I love going to the horse races whenever I can.

THE HIGH-STAKES SOFTBALL GAME: AN UNEXPECTED RIDE WITH FREE SPIRITS

Besides working at Ruidoso Downs, I wanted to join a softball team for the summer. I had been playing softball since I was seven years old, and a summer hadn't gone by that I didn't play. I was eating at a local Mexican restaurant when I asked the waitress if there were any softball teams in the area. She said she was on a softball team. I gave her my number and told her if they ever needed an extra player to give me a call. Within a few days, she called me and said they needed a first baseman. I immediately said, "Yes!" They were going to pick me up in front of the Mexican restaurant.

There were five women in the car. I hopped in and away we went up the mountain towards the softball field. I was in the back seat, in the middle, wedged between two women. Immediately, I thought that these women really like to have fun. The car windows were down and their long dark hair was flying everywhere. When we were halfway up the mountain, I realized that the women were stoned. By this point, it was too late to get out of the car. There were times that the driver got so close to veering off the road and there were no guardrails.

However, I knew there was nothing I could do so I sat back, relaxed, and trusted that everything would be okay.

Miraculously, we reached the softball field and won the game and made it down the mountain safely! They only needed me for one day, but I'll never forget them and how they included me, brought me on their team without knowing me, and treated me like I was part of the group. We waved goodbye and I never saw them again.

CHAPTER 4

WALKING IN MY DAD'S FOOTSTEPS

A father holds his daughter's hand for a short while,
but he holds her heart forever.
—UNKNOWN

Growing up, I was practically my dad's shadow as we enjoyed short jaunts to the hardware store or any other errand he was running. We loved going to classic car shows together, so I was super excited to eventually get my driver's license.

I took my driver's test for the first time on my sixteenth birthday. I was so excited to drive! I had to parallel park between two poles while driving my dad's 1970 blue Chrysler Plymouth. When I backed up, I hit one of the poles. The driving instructor told me that I failed. I explained to him that I just hit a pole. He said, "You hit a car." I said, "Oh." The next day, my dad and I practiced parallel parking.

The second time I took the driving test, I passed. When I first began driving, my dad started to put the sign of the cross on my forehead with his finger. And without fail, whenever I would leave the house as I got older and more experienced, he would come up to me, draw the sign of the cross on my forehead, and say goodbye.

A FATHER'S GIFT: STEERING THROUGH GRIEF AND GUILT

About a year after getting my driver's license, I was driving my mother home from the grocery store. In our neighborhood, a young boy dashed out in front of our car without looking both ways. I slammed on the brakes and came to a sudden stop. My mother and I breathed a sigh of relief that everyone was okay and no one was hurt. As I drove forward about six feet, the boy's dog ran in front of us out of nowhere as the wheels were moving. I heard a thud, and we stopped and got out of the car. It was obvious that the dog was hurt.

The dog's owner was there. They said that their dog darted out in the streets often and they were worried that this might happen. I nervously and quietly drove home with tears in my eyes. We found out later that night that the dog died. I cried for days about the dog. My sixteen-year-old self didn't know how to grieve over this. At school, the boy who owned the dog told classmates that I ran over his dog.

After several days of crying, being sad, and refusing to ever drive again, my dad came into my bedroom. He brought me three red roses. I had never seen flowers in our house before. I wondered where he got the three roses. I sat up in my bed and he handed me the flowers. He told me that I had to get back on the horse again. He said that I had to get behind the wheel and start driving again. If I didn't, I would regret not having the experience of driving myself places and being independent. At that moment, I got out of bed and put my roses in a cup with water. We then went out to the car, and I drove him around the block until I felt comfortable driving again.

Years later, after the hijacking and experiencing being a hostage and shot in the head, I knew it was important to get back on a plane again, or to get back on the horse again as my dad put it. I knew if I didn't fly again, I would regret not going to places I wanted to visit. He was absolutely right.

DINNER WITH DAD

One weekend, my sisters Gloria and Mary and I went over to my parents' house for dinner. It was a Saturday evening. My father made us fried chicken, mashed potatoes, gravy, and green beans. It was one of my most favorite meals that he'd make for us. We were all seated at the kitchen table. As we started passing around the platter of fried chicken, my sisters and I started asking questions about the chicken. As we held up the parts of the chicken we asked, "Is this a thigh? Is this a breast? Is this a drumstick? Which one has the white meat, and which is the dark meat?" It ended up being quite a conversation as we attempted to figure all of this out. That's when all hell broke loose.

I didn't realize how frustrating the conversation was to my dad. He pounded his fist on the table and shouted, "Gosh dang it, there's two things I wish for you girls. First, learn the parts of the chicken and second, get somebody else to work on your cars other than me! That's what I want for all of you."

I looked up from my plate a little shocked and continued eating while I worked to sustain my giggles as best I could. I knew he was thinking since we were in our twenties, we should know the parts of a chicken and perhaps keep our cars tuned up. I remember thinking,

Gosh, I hope he wants more for us than knowing the parts of a chicken and finding someone to work on our cars.

THIRTY DAYS AT A TIME: CHERISHING MY FATHER'S LEGACY

When my mom and dad were in their eighties, my mom passed away. My dad became lonely, and his memory started to fail. I was living out of state in Minnesota, and he was in Texas. I decided to visit him monthly and stay for five days. I made plans to fly from Minneapolis to Houston each month and stay with him in the house he lived in, which was the same house that I grew up in. One morning, I laid out his pills for him to take for the day. He refused to take them. "I'm not going to take these pills," he said. I told him that he really needed to take his pills.

I gave him all sorts of reasons why it was important for him to take his medicine, but, for some reason, he was refusing to do so that morning. After a few minutes of arguing back and forth about the pills, I said to him, "Dad, you have fought in two wars and survived to talk about it, I'm pretty sure you can take these pills." He said, "Really? I've been in two wars?"

I said, "Yes, you were in World War II and the Korean War."

He said, "Well, isn't that something!" I responded, "Yes, that's definitely something!" As he took his pills, I told him about how he loved serving in the Navy and the stories he told me as I was growing up. For ten years, I visited my dad every thirty days. By making that commitment, I was able to live with no regrets when my dad passed away. It showed me the importance of spending time with people I care about. The time I spent with him was immeasurable.

We would spend our days hanging out, going to some doctors' appointments, going for walks, going to lunch, watching television, making dinner at home, driving around, and talking about stories from his childhood. I shared his love for classic cars, so we took much joy in visiting car museums. He could look at any classic car and tell you what year it was. At one point, I bought a 1963 white Chevy pickup truck that I named after my dad, Eugene.

His dad passed away from meningitis when he was six years old and his mother, my grandma Nora Nink, moved her three small children to Smithville, Texas, to stay with her family where they lived until my dad joined the Navy at the age of seventeen. A few years later, he met my mother Rylma in Seattle where they were both stationed. They eventually left the military and moved to Houston, Texas, where they raised their three daughters (including me!).

One morning, I got a phone call from my family letting me know it was time for me to come to Houston even though I had just returned a few days before from my monthly visit. At the age of ninety-three, my dad was getting worse. Alzheimer's had taken its toll on him. I quickly hopped on a plane from Minneapolis to Houston and took an Uber to see my dad in the memory care facility. When the Uber driver dropped me off, I grabbed my bags and went into his room.

Everybody was there including my sisters, nephew, and his wife. There was a hospice nurse in the corner, and they were all talking amongst themselves when I walked in and approached my dad's bed. There were no chairs left so I laid down next to him on his bed and started talking to him, whispering in his ear. As I was talking to him, his frail body, which was very still, started to shake uncontrollably. My niece Alayna yelled out in an excited voice, "He was waiting for you to come. He was waiting for you to get here. He's responding. He knows you're here now. He's been waiting for you! The hospice nurse said he might react to the voices of people he knows."

Meanwhile, I kept talking to him. I told him that his three daughters, his three grandchildren, and three great-grandchildren would be okay. I whispered in his ear that he was the light of my life. I thanked him for showing up for me and having my back, for being the role model he was and the role model that I needed, and for being my forever cheerleader.

For the last time, I took his tired right hand and drew the sign of the cross with his finger on my forehead and told him I loved him. I kissed him and said goodbye. Within three hours of my arrival, he passed. After my dad's funeral, I thought about his legacy and what he left behind. He was the perfect example of living his life from the goodness of his heart, living with Grace, and always doing the right thing. I miss him. I was incredibly blessed to learn from him for sixty-three years.

When I look back, I realize how my dad always encouraged my sense of adventure even when I went *way* outside my comfort zone.

CHAPTER 5

LEARNING TO LET GO

To let go does not mean to get rid of.
To let go means to let be. When we let be with compassion,
things come and go on their own.
—JACK KORNFIELD, *THE ART OF FORGIVENESS,
LOVINGKINDNESS, AND PEACE*

When I was sixty-one, my son graduated from high school. He left to attend Creighton University in Omaha, Nebraska, a six-hour drive from our home in Minneapolis. I was clueless as to what to do without him. I had raised this amazing young man who was more than ready to move away and experience life on his own. Of course, I wanted him to grow up and lead an independent life; however, the idea of letting go was bittersweet and emotionally challenging. I cried several times a day for three weeks.

What I was experiencing reminded me of the movie *Otherhood*. In the movie, Angela Bassett, Patricia Arquette, and Felicity Huffman decide to drive to New York to reconnect with their adult sons. Their trip becomes a journey of rediscovery that forces these women to redefine their relationships with their children, friends, spouses, and most importantly, themselves. Angela Bassett's character tells her son that she needs to find out who she is without him because her life was so intertwined with his; her son had successfully found out who he was without her, but she had not done the same. This movie spoke to me because, as a mother, I let my life intertwine with my son's a bit too much. My days, nights, and weekends of going to his school events, soccer games, and basketball games were now over, and, like Bassett's character, I needed to find out who I was without my son.

It was a silly feeling, but it felt like someone broke up with me. I found myself on a journey to finding out who I was without him, whether I liked it or not. Certainly, I continued to travel and do things with friends while he was growing up, but I was emotionally intertwined with him. I loved that I was emotionally connected with him, but I also loved how I learned to find out who I was without him.

It took me a while to find my way, but after a year, I started to make the adjustments. The empty nest experience is a time of grieving over the way it was, making way for a new purpose, a new beginning, and a new transition in life. I remember watching the movie *How Do You Know*, where Reese Witherspoon portrays the main character Lisa.

She goes to see a psychologist to help her with an issue she's dealing with. Because her insurance only covered her one initial visit, she knew she wouldn't be going back. She asked the psychologist if there was just one thing he could tell his clients, what would it be? He responded, "Figure out what you want and then find a way to make it happen." It's like writing a bucket list and then checking them off one by one.

After Tanner went to college, I visited the Christmas markets in Europe for a few days in December, traded my car in for a convertible so I could experience the beautiful Minnesota summers by being outside while I was driving, and began writing this book. All these things were on my bucket list, things I dreamed about for a long time, but didn't do. My son has now graduated from college and is working as a teacher. In *Otherhood*, at the end of the movie, Angela Bassett goes to Paris to paint, which was a long-time dream of hers. She successfully found a way to find out who she was and what she wanted for herself.

As I have gone through twists and turns in my life—the miscarriage, the hijacking where I was shot in the head, colon cancer, divorce, the empty nest challenge—I've learned to remind myself to never give up. I've learned if you stay with it, the feelings of loneliness, and not knowing what to do eventually pass and you find angels who show up for you and help make life better. I needed to experience the empty nest syndrome so I could start paying attention to what was best for me and to continue to make sure that happiness, joy, and excitement stayed a part of my life.

FINDING JOY IN CHALLENGES: EMBRACING LOVE AND LAUGHTER THROUGH LIFE'S SETBACKS

In June of 2018, my niece Alayna and her daughter, my great-niece, Vega, came to visit me in Minneapolis. The day before they came, I was walking down the stairs in my house to go to the laundry room. I missed a step, fell down the stairs, and broke my right foot. I couldn't believe that I did this the day before they were to visit.

I had reserved tickets to see the musical *Mama Mia!* at the Chanhassen Dinner Theatres, bought tickets to the horse races at Canterbury Park, bought tickets to see Carrie Underwood along with a tour of the US Bank Stadium where the Minnesota Vikings play. In short, much thought, time, and money had gone into planning their visit, and I knew in my heart a broken foot would disrupt it all. The doctor fit me for a boot and told me not to put any pressure on my foot. I was to use crutches or a wheelchair to get around for the next couple of weeks. I not only cried because I fell down the stairs but because of the incredible pain I was in and the idea that Alayna and Vega might not be able to visit the next day.

I called Alayna and told her what happened and that I didn't want them to cancel their trip. She and I talked about how we were going to get through the next eight days. She would drive my car and take us everywhere. We would take breaks and rest often and take my wheelchair with us wherever we went. With this plan in place, we were looking forward to enjoying our time together.

One day during their visit, they wanted to go to the Mall of America. That morning, I was feeling tired, and my foot was hurting more than usual. I told them to take my car and go by themselves. As soon as they drove off, I regretted it. I don't get the chance to see them that often because they live so far away, so I wanted to make the most of spending as much time with them as possible. After thirty minutes of wishing I had gone with them, I called Alayna and told her I had changed my mind. I got a ride to the mall and met them at the location they chose—I'm so glad I let go, made the call, and met up with them that day.

We had lunch, went shopping, and laughed as they pushed me through the Mall of America in my wheelchair. Vega made sure my foot was propped up and I was comfortable. At one point, Alayna was holding onto my wheelchair while I was in it. She accidentally let go and I started to roll away into the crowd. Vega scolded her mom, saying it was important to take care of Aunt Jackie. When we were home, Vega lectured me on how I needed to stay off my foot, sit or lie down, and keep my leg higher than the level of my heart to reduce the swelling. For eight days, she watched over me. She and her mom Alayna were the ones who stepped up to the plate and took on the responsibility to take care of me.

When the date of the Carrie Underwood concert arrived, we were ready. Inside the concert venue, the Target Center, we stopped at the desk and were able to exchange our tickets for seats that were in an area where there weren't as many stairs to climb.

Vega pushed me around in my wheelchair and took care of me while Alayna began to lead our pack to find our seats. When we arrived near our seats, the agent explained to us that we needed to leave my wheelchair with him, alongside the other wheelchairs that were left. Alayna and Vega became concerned. Alayna explained to the agent that the wheelchair needed to be available for us when it was time to leave. He assured her that would happen. When the concert was over, we sat in our seats and made sure the crowds were gone before we made our way down the stairs to get my wheelchair. When we got there, my wheelchair was gone.

There was a wheelchair there, but Alayna explained to the agent that it wasn't mine. I looked at it. *How did she know so quickly that it wasn't mine?* At first, I wondered if it mattered. It was late, I was extremely tired, and I wanted to go home. I began to notice things about the wheelchair. It was a little beat up compared to mine. Then I remembered that I needed to make sure I returned the one I rented back to the rental store. The agent got on his walkie-talkie to find out where my wheelchair was. One of the workers had used it to take someone to their car and was on his way back. Relief flooded through us, and when we eventually returned back to my home, we got a late-night snack and reminisced about our day noting how funny and cute it was that Alayna was the mama bear to me and my wheelchair that night.

During their trip, there were days when we lied around the house, watched their favorite television shows, made chocolate chip cookies, played cards, and used Vega's phone making funny faces on Snapchat. I laughed and laughed. As the eight days with them flew by, it was time for them to go home all too soon. When they left, I began to think about our whirlwind trip that we agreed to continue anyway and how Vega and Alayna, out of the blue, became the angels I needed. I will be forever grateful.

FROM CLASSROOM TO STAGE: GIVING UP ONE CAREER FOR ANOTHER

Giving up my teaching career was difficult. I had to let go because the repercussions of my head injury had started to get in the way of my teaching. After being shot, I was now reading at a first-grade level and finding it hard to keep up.

I knew it was time to let it go and embrace new opportunities. About three years after the hijacking, I began my career as a motivational speaker. It started small, but eventually, I shared the stage with the likes of Terry Bradshaw, Colin Powell, Anita Hill, and Larry King.

Before becoming a professional speaker, I shied away from telling my story about the hijacking for a very long time. It was a story that hurt me deeply. I didn't know exactly what I was going to talk about on the stage. As I began to learn some lessons from the hijacking, I started to feel comfortable telling my story to a group. Whether I was ready or not, the motivational business career of Jackie Pflug and Associates had begun.

At first, it felt like the business was dragging me along as the business world definitely was not in my wheelhouse. I loved being an educator because I was trained as an educator. I felt most at home being a teacher and educational diagnostician—you could ask me almost anything about bringing along a student that was behind and how to get them caught up to their grade level. I knew how to communicate with children and their parents in a way that made them feel calm, but I didn't know much about anything to do with owning a business.

BUILDING A BUSINESS FROM COURAGE AND COLD CALLS

As the weeks and months went by, I came to understand that not having a deep understanding in business was a hindrance, but not a necessity on my part. I realized quickly to lean on others who knew the world of small business and relied on them heavily. My close friend Mark LeBlanc, author of *Growing Your Business!: What You Need to Know What You Need to Do*, became my mentor and driving force in my business. I did everything he told me to do with an excitement that perhaps I could have a successful business where I could enjoy myself, make some money, and at the same time share the valuable lessons I learned from the hard experience I had of being a hostage and living with a brain injury. Mark's marketing plan was intense and required making ten cold calls per day. That took a lot of gumption and the ability to let go of whatever happened on those calls. But I did it knowing that's what I needed to do to become successful in my business.

THE POWER OF ONE: HOW A SINGLE CALL IMPACTED MY SPEAKING CAREER

I began reading books that I thought would help me in this journey of learning what business was all about. I had read the book *Don't Sweat the Small Stuff... and It's All Small Stuff: Simple Ways to Keep the Little Things from Taking Over Your Life* by Richard Carlson, PhD, years before and found its lessons useful for stress management. So, when his book, *Don't Sweat the Small Stuff at Work: Simple Ways to Minimize Stress and Conflict* was published, I decided that it might help me. The one thing that struck me as I was reading it was the idea of doing "one thing" every day that would help with your business. The one thing can't be emptying the dishwasher or putting away your clothes into the dryer from the washer—it has to be one thing that will help your business.

I had a thought. Since I have epilepsy from the gunshot wound to my head, I always wanted to speak to the National Epilepsy Foundation. I had been speaking to local epilepsy foundations, but I had always wanted to speak at the annual event. I decided that calling someone at the National Epilepsy Foundation was going to be my one thing that I was going to do that particular day for my business. I found out what the director's name was and nervously made the call. I told him my name and that I had spoken to the Epilepsy Foundation of Minnesota a few years before and wanted to know if I might be a good fit as a speaker for their upcoming national convention or perhaps a future national convention. He politely said no.

We talked for a few more minutes and then hung up. Disappointedly, I thought, *Shoot, I really wanted to speak at their convention.* Despite the rejection, I still felt successful because I did one thing that day that I thought might boost my speaking career. I began thinking about what my one thing might be for tomorrow, when my phone rang. It was the director of the National Epilepsy Foundation again. I thought he had changed his mind, but he was calling to ask me what medication I was on to control my seizures. I told him I was taking Tegretol -XR to control my seizures.

He began to tell me that he was reading some of his mail and he came across a letter from Novartis Pharmaceuticals Corporation, the company that makes Tegretol -XR. Novartis was looking for a spokesperson for Tegretol -XR, someone who was taking the medication and having success. He gave me their phone number. I called the number of the person who was spearheading the project. Within a few weeks, I was hired as the spokesperson for Tegretol -XR. I made one call. That one call turned into a very big thing for my business. From that point on, I examined any thought that came to me. If I felt an urge, an idea, or a push to do something, I followed it. I listened.

WRAPPING UP MY SPEAKING CAREER

After twenty-five years of speaking on stage about my story and valuable lessons learned, I was getting a feeling that it was coming to an end. That wasn't something I wanted to acknowledge because I really did love speaking. I loved the people I met, I loved the hotels I stayed in, the comfortable beds I slept in, and feeling like I was making a difference. The message I was getting was that I had done my part and that it was time to take a rest. I fought the feeling for a couple of years, still speaking at conferences and telling my story.

As time went on, I could tell that my heart wanted to go somewhere else, to a new project perhaps. I stopped booking myself on future speaking engagements and fulfilled the last remaining speeches on my calendar. My last speech was to an automotive convention in Las Vegas on May 11, 2011. My friend Debbie came to watch me speak on stage for the last time; it was time to let go, and this was a fitting end.

I am grateful I listened to my intuition on this major life decision; in fact, I welcomed it. Tanner was in middle school at the time, and I was excited to walk him to the bus and not need to rush to catch a flight immediately to go to work. Truthfully, I never thought of myself as retiring, just simply ceasing my speaking at conferences. But by ending my speaking career, it gave me time and space to visit my dad and spend quality time with Tanner.

As time went on, my friend Marcia Behring decided to retire from teaching; I wanted to know what she was going to do with her time. I thought perhaps it would give me guidance on how to spend my time without working. She came up with the acronym M.O.V.E. to help with the transition into retirement. M: make some money; O: look for opportunities; V: volunteer; and E: exercise.

She decided to embrace this acronym because shortly after she retired from teaching, she wasn't sure who she was anymore. She was always a teacher and didn't know how to go on without teaching. She wanted to re-identify herself, who she was, and what she wanted to focus on. She didn't want to flounder around, so she developed a course of action—M.O.V.E.

Her M.O.V.E. inspired her to take a job outside her comfort zone. She helped open a kitchen shop and worked in retail. She wanted to create opportunities for new learning. In addition, she learned how to make pottery, play the ukulele, line dance, play canasta, and do yoga. She, in turn, inspired me to look carefully into the day-to-day things I was doing to make sure I was moving toward joy.

CUTTING THE CORD: HOW VISUALIZATION HELPED ME LET GO

I see my chiropractor Dr. Michael Isaacson ideally every other week. I've been doing that for years and it's part of my self-care. It helps keep me aligned and it makes me feel good. Several years ago, Dr. Mike told me that I had a recording in my mind of the hijacking that was playing over and over again. I wondered how he knew that, but as I carefully thought about it, he was right. For many years, without really being aware of it, I had been replaying the hijacking over and over in my head several times a day. How could that be? I couldn't believe it! *Why was I doing that? Surely, that can't be good for me, continuously replaying that event in my head*, I thought. I started to pay attention to what I was doing.

If I saw an airplane, the tape started to play from the beginning of the hijacking to the end of the hijacking, from getting on the aircraft to being shot. If I was going through security at an airport, the recording or tape began. It played inside my head even if I was at home watching television, talking to someone, or making dinner. I was in shock when I realized what I was doing to myself.

Dr. Mike told me that I needed to cut the cord. I nodded because I knew that I needed to stop the tape from playing. I wasn't sure how to cut the cord—I asked Dr. Mike how I was supposed to do that. He said that I needed to figure that out on my own.

As I left his office, an idea came to me. I sat in the front seat of my car, locked the doors, and closed my eyes. I started to visualize or picture a cord (like an umbilical cord) going from my belly button to a large balloon floating in the air. The balloon contained the entire hijacking, from beginning to end. From when I got on the plane to when I was shot, to when I was thrown off the plane onto the tarmac. All the emotions of being terrified, hurt, and lost, along with thinking I was going to die, were in the balloon. I was careful to add everything I could think of relating to the hijacking in this balloon. With my eyes still closed, my left hand took a hold of the imaginary balloon as my right pointer and middle finger became a pair of scissors. Before I cut the cord, I told the things in the balloon that I appreciated it being in my life and I loved how it taught me so many things about myself and the lessons I learned from it, but it was time to let go. Holding on to those memories was starting to affect my health.

With thanks in my heart, I began to cut the imaginary cord right near my belly button with my imaginary finger scissors. I visualized the cord detaching from me. I visualized the balloon and cord drifting up the sky and into the heavens until I could no longer see it in my mind's eye. I smiled, started my car, and drove away. I could immediately tell something had shifted.

The next week when I saw Dr. Mike, I told him what I did and how now when I think about the hijacking, I can think about the part I'm thinking about without going from beginning to end with the tape.

Cutting the cord was a lesson in letting go for me. Since then, I have used that same technique in letting go of experiences or challenges that my mind wants to think about over and over.

LETTING GO OF THE DREAM

In January of 2024, I sold my house that I loved and had lived in since 1994. There were so many memories there as it was the house where my son grew up; it was actually one of the hardest things I had done. I knew it was necessary to move forward during my transformation, but incredibly sad and difficult too. It took some time to process that sadness. I tend to get attached to the things that I own, to the car I drive, to the clothes that I wear, to the friends that I make. Letting go of my house was part of the process of grieving the part of me that no longer worked. I loved that house, it provided happiness, memories, and a safe place to fall.

But by selling it, it made room for something else even though I didn't know what that something else was going to be. The same applies to letting go of a friendship that no longer serves you, it is bittersweet. Bitter is the grief we feel while sweet is about the joy in the fact that it happened. I had a challenging time with being sorry that my time with my house was over, instead of focusing on being happy that the time I was in that house with my family had actually happened.

I needed to make some big changes in my life and didn't really know what that would look like and I wasn't sure I was ready for it . . . but I let go and embraced the bittersweet change all the same.

CHAPTER 6

WHEN ONE DOOR CLOSES, ANOTHER OPENS

Sometimes the hardest doors to close are the
ones you never wanted to open.

—UNKNOWN

When we lose something, we have to open the next door or we run
the chance of getting lost, feeling unhappy, or unfulfilled. Sometimes
finding that open door can be a challenge simply because we find
ourselves getting busy with things that don't really matter. In this
age of social media, it's easy to get lost and forget to focus on what
really matters most. Family has always really mattered to me, and I
do what I can to stay connected.

CAMP AUNT JACKIE: PLANNING THE ULTIMATE
SUMMER VACATION FOR MY NEPHEWS

My nephew Michael (Mike) and his wife Susan have two sons, Marshall and Owen.

When they were born, I told Mike that when the boys got to a certain age, that I wanted them to spend time with me in Minnesota. When Marshall was eight and Owen was six, Mike thought they might be ready. I was surprised, yet so happy.

The plan was that Mike would fly them from their hometown in Austin, Texas, to Minneapolis. Mike would stay for a couple of days, then fly back home to Austin while the boys would stay with me, Tanner, and my husband at the time. At the end of the trip, Mike would fly back up to Minnesota, stay for a day, and then fly with the boys back home.

I carefully planned that first summer visit, knowing how important it was to do so. I wanted them to have so much fun that they would beg their parents to come back again the next summer. At the beginning, the boys stayed for five days, then the next year it was seven days, then it evolved to fourteen days.

I planned to do two things a day with them. And if we were out and about during the day and needed to stop and have lunch, that lunch did not count as one of the two things.

Our list of activities was expansive. We played mini golf, painted ceramics, went to movies, went to the zoo, went to the Imax theater, the horse races, trampoline centers, Mall of America, saw a musical, and improv at the Chanhassen Dinner Theatres, enjoyed the parks, went swimming in pools and lakes, and the list went on and on.

In fact, I kept a copy of the list of our activities so I could refer back to it and then add new activities throughout the year. I can't explain the joy I got planning the activities and being with them.

Someone told me something like this couldn't be done; that the boys would get homesick and want to go home after the first day. Instead of choosing the kind of talk that would uplift and support me during this time, I was hearing negative talk. Nevertheless, I couldn't have been happier, and nothing was going to stop me from having the time of my life.

The boys started to call our time together Camp Aunt Jackie, and, to have a little fun, I began having T-shirts made for each visit that said "Camp Aunt Jackie, Minnesota" and the year. This was made easy by my friend Elsa who makes the T-shirts, and every year she gets more creative with them! To immortalize, and as a finishing touch to their much-anticipated annual visits, after they leave, I make a photo album of their time with me and mail it to them.

Now, in 2024 as I write this, Marshall is fifteen and Owen is thirteen, and they are still coming to see me every year; this has become the highlight of my summer.

CAMP AUNT JACKIE: A PROMISE OF FUN
INTERRUPTED BY A SUDDEN DEPARTURE

One summer, a few years ago, Vega wanted to join Camp Aunt Jackie with her cousins. I had invited her every year to join us, but she said she wasn't ready. That particular summer, she said yes. All of us were beaming from ear to ear that we had a new person joining our fun little summer heaven of laughing, giggling, telling jokes, playing cards and games, and just being with and loving family.

I had the T-shirts made and laid out on the beds. Mike flew Marshall, Owen, and Vega from Austin, stayed for one night and left early the next morning. The day was going to be jam packed with activities. We scoured the shelves for our favorite candy at Minnesota's Largest Candy Store, stopped at the annual Chaska River

City Days festival in Chaska, ate delicious dipped-in-mustard corn dogs, listened to loud and lively country music, went swimming, and played pool and ping pong. It was now 5:00 pm and I started making my usual spaghetti with meat sauce, succulent summer sweet corn, fresh cucumber salad, and perfectly toasted garlic bread for dinner.

We sat down, said our prayers, and began to visit about what we were going to do on our second day. Marshall, Owen, Tanner, and Vega agreed that we would go to the Mall of America to ride the rides and stop by Dairy Queen on the way home. As everyone continued to eat, the phone rang. It was Mike.

Mike and his wife Susan had flown to Cannon Beach, Oregon, to spend time together while the boys were with me. They had just arrived at their hotel when they got a voicemail from the camp one of the boys had attended prior to coming to me. It turned out one of the bus drivers had been diagnosed with COVID-19. They wanted me to check on their son. He was eating his spaghetti, and he looked good, was laughing, and had lots of energy. I was sure that everything would work out fine.

An hour later, the dishes, pots, and pans were put away. I had promised Vega that I would make chocolate chip cookies with her after dinner. As we were getting the measuring cups, spoons, pans, and ingredients out, I told her that I would be right back. I went upstairs to check on my nephew once again.

He was in his room playing video games. His face was now swollen and red and he had a fever. I called Mike and said that I was going to take him in to see a doctor and to get him tested. It turned out he had Covid. Within twelve hours, Mike had flown from Oregon to Minneapolis on a red eye flight through the night, rented a car, and was at my house at 6:30 a.m.

I told the boys the night before that their dad was going to need to bring them home so their parents could take care of them, and as we sleepily walked them to the rental car parked in the driveway at 6:45 a.m., everyone was tired and not feeling well. Getting into the back seat, Owen said, "Does this mean that we're not going to the Mall of America today? Does this mean we're not going to Dairy Queen today?" I said, "Yes, that's what this means. I'm so sorry, but I promise you that we'll do a do-over." Doing do-overs was something Tanner and I did often as he was growing up. If we didn't like what we said to the other person or we didn't like how we acted or the day didn't go as we had planned, we asked for a do-over. Giving Owen the opportunity to have a do-over came to my mind instantly. By the afternoon, Vega was gone as well. The house was empty, and I was only able to spend one full day with them instead of the originally anticipated fourteen days.

FROM TEARS TO TRANSFORMATION: ASKING FOR HELP

I was devastated. I began to cry and cry and cry. I couldn't stop crying for days. Tanner began to worry about me, saying, "Mom, I don't like seeing you like this." I couldn't remember the last time I cried this much. Perhaps when Tanner went off to college. But this cry was different. It seemed deeper and much more sorrow was in its steady stream of tears. It was about something I couldn't seem to understand or put my finger on.

I decided that I needed to find a way to understand what this was about. I was extremely depressed and felt lost after my nephews left so suddenly from Camp Aunt Jackie and I couldn't stop crying. I knew I needed to get help. When it all fell apart, I wasn't sure what to do with all the emotions that were coming my way. Something inside, my Inner Voice, suggested I go to a retreat center of some kind to get assistance with healing from this event. A dream of mine for a very long time was to go to a certain retreat center in Tucson, Arizona. I noticed that I was getting emails from them out of the blue and a message from my Inner Voice said that it was time to go for a visit.

Just five days later, I called the center and booked my stay for six nights. I chose a room that had a little more bells and whistles to it. I thought that was what I needed to pamper myself.

KICKED OUT BY FATE: A JOURNEY OF TRANSFORMATION SET IN MOTION

It was 10:00 p.m. Arizona time and midnight Central time when I arrived in Tucson, and I was exhausted from my long, and delayed, flights. I checked in and someone took me to my room. It was a beautiful room with a substantial bathtub, an outside patio overlooking the mountains, a fountain, and a hot tub.

I immediately knew the room felt too big for the journey I was embarking on for the next seven days. Things started to go wrong. The curtains wouldn't close due to the heat and the door wouldn't lock. I called maintenance and they came immediately to fix the curtains and lock. As the maintenance man left, I thought of a quick question I wanted to ask him. I opened the door to look outside and as I did that, the door closed and locked very quickly behind me. It felt like the room was telling me something, almost like it was kicking me out.

The maintenance man was long gone, and I didn't have any shoes on because I had taken them off in the room, nor did I have my cell phone with me. I had already unpacked my suitcase as well; it's a good thing that I still had my clothes on. It was extremely dark outside. As I walked down a dark and unfamiliar path, I was confused on which direction to go. The sidewalk under my feet was rough. I walked for twenty minutes in the dark when I started to cry. It had been such a long day traveling and my emotions were raw. I was hoping a golf cart would come by and rescue me, but it never happened.

After thirty minutes of walking in the dark, it was almost 1:00 a.m., which was 3:00 a.m. my time. I decided to knock on someone's door for help. I was nervous because it was so late, and I didn't want to scare anyone. I saw a light on in one of the rooms; I decided to knock on their door for help. A woman on the other side of the door said, "Who is it?" I explained that I got locked out of my room and could she call someone to come get me outside of her room. Within minutes, someone on a golf cart came to my rescue and delivered me to the front desk.

There, I saw Kristina again who had checked me in earlier. With tears in my eyes, I told her that I got locked out. I also told her that I wanted a different room, a room that was much smaller. I knew when I first entered the original room that it was much too big for me. I had decided that I was just going to stay there anyway because I had already unpacked my suitcase, that it would be too much of a hassle and it was so late. But then I got locked out and I knew I needed to say something. She found me a smaller room. She went back with me in the wee hours of the night to help me pack up my suitcase and move rooms.

Sometimes things might become a hassle, and we feel it's just better not to say what's on our mind or be in our own corner or listen to our Inner Voice. I have to say that when my original room kicked me out, I was able to see the beautiful stars while I was crying and met a very kind woman that lent me a helping hand. I realized that it's important to listen to the ideas and messages flowing through us and speak up.

I went to a retreat center that I had been wanting to go to for years but didn't go for one reason or another. I was there for a few days and came back quiet, centered, and at peace. I was able to work through my sadness and heal somewhat. I knew the crying wasn't about the boys and Vega leaving abruptly. It was about something inside of me that needed to come out. This was the beginning of my big transformation, little did I know.

The next summer came and Tanner, Marshall, Owen, and I were excited to have our Camp Aunt Jackie. I soaked in the love, fun, and laughter. When they left in August, I went back to the retreat center. This time, I went back to learn more about myself and what was needed in my life. When I returned home, I felt strong, and I knew that changes needed to take place for me to live a consistent life of happiness, joy, and laughter. It was time to work on myself.

THE BROKEN PLATE: HOW LIFE'S ACCIDENTS LEAD TO LOVE'S DESIGN

In season four, episode one of the popular television show *This is Us*, there is a scene where a blind musician is at his home making scrambled eggs for breakfast. As he is sitting down to eat his eggs, his dog jumps on him and knocks the plate out of his hands. The plate breaks into pieces. The young man moves his dog out of the way and begins to pick up the broken pieces of the plate and puts them on the kitchen counter.

In the next scene, the young man is walking into a café to have breakfast. A beautiful woman leads him to an empty booth. A few minutes go by, and the young man invites the waitress to sit down.

They exchange words and he asks to hold her hands. By the look on his face, you could tell that he had found someone he could love.

The young man goes back to his apartment and remembers the broken plate. He immediately begins writing a song about his encounter. If the plate hadn't broken, he wouldn't have gone out for breakfast that morning to that café and he wouldn't have had the exchange with the young woman.

As the scenes go on, they date, get married, and she becomes pregnant with their child. During the last scene, the camera pans over to the wall where the young blind man had glued the pieces of the plate to make it whole, framed it, and hung it on the wall.

I smiled as I saw that. To me, that plate was a reminder that even though something may break and perhaps get in the way or get us down, it might be the one thing that helps us find a new path, the one thing that could lead us to something incredible. Perhaps it's God's way of doing a God wink and turning something insignificant or irritating like breaking a plate into something that could be glorious.

Good comes from what appears to be bad.

CHAPTER 7

FROM FAMILIAR TO FEARLESS

A Journey of Transformation

Sometimes to survive, we must become more
than we were programmed to be.
—THE WILD ROBOT FILM

Back in 2010, I was at the movie theater watching *Eat, Pray, Love*. It was the end of the movie and right before the credits rolled, I was just starting to stand up when Julia Roberts's character Liz said something profound. I immediately sat down as I listened intently to these words:

In the end, I've come to believe in something I call the 'physics of the quest,' a force in nature governed by the laws of gravity. The rules of quest physics goes something like this: If you're brave enough to leave behind everything familiar and comforting and set out on a truth seeking journey either internally or externally, and if you are truly willing to regard everything that happens to you on that journey as a clue and if you accept everyone you meet along the way as a teacher and if you are prepared most of all to face and forgive some of the most difficult realities about yourself, then the truth will not be withheld from you.

I wanted to hear those words again because I related to them so deeply. Since there was no streaming newly released movies back then, I bought another movie ticket. And even though those words certainly resonated with the hijacking and my recovery journey, they applied even more with my most recent life challenges.

Change is hard, but so rewarding. I had compromised my reality and values for so long that I needed someone or something to pull me out of it and wake me up. For me, a retreat center was the answer I was seeking. Little did I know that when I went there, I was about to learn some transformative tools that could help me make some significant changes in my life. Before I share some of these tools and my journey, I want to say that not everybody needs to go to a retreat center to transform themselves, it just happened to be the answer I was looking for. But, more importantly, it all starts with a desire to change from within—that's all it is.

CREATING LASTING CHANGE AND A LIFE OF INTENTION

As I look at making changes in my life and living a life of intention, I want connections with people that I can trust and who want to love me and be playful with me. I want to feel inspired. I want to feel peaceful and present and not so much in my head. I ask myself, "Am I putting myself in a position where that can happen or am I inside my house watching TV day in and day out? I want to feel peaceful and present. Am I doing exercises or working with others that help me move to a life of being peaceful and present or am I doing the same thing over and over again that moves me away from my peace by overreacting and getting upset about something someone might have said?"

In order to create clarity, we must align our thoughts with our actions. We need to ask ourselves tough questions to find that clarity. We need to look at what we need to stop being afraid of, what we need to improve, spend more time on, spend less time on, and what we want to learn. Then, we have to look at how that will ideally make us feel.

Creating a life of intention and living our authentic life is created by awareness and action and creating realistic expectations. We no longer have to wait around anymore for others to take action. Instead, we empower ourselves.

I can say to myself, "Even though my social life is not where I want it to be, I am so grateful for the relationships I have. Even though I'm feeling overwhelmed today, I'm grateful for the apartment I live in and the great Mexican meal I had last night."

Doing work on ourselves is not for the weak of heart. When I wake up in the morning, I have to be intentional about living my values and choosing to be around people that are uplifting and positive. I don't want to be around negative people that pull me down. That takes a lot of work. I was in danger of getting to the point of not recognizing myself if I didn't wake up to life. I'm so glad I woke up.

81

ALWAYS RESPECT INTUITION

During the spring and summer of 2017, I was extremely sick with respiratory issues. I had been dealing with it for a couple of years before, but it was getting worse. I tried everything I could think of to get healthy and saw doctor after doctor and nothing worked. One doctor said he just didn't know what else to try. It continued to get worse with time. I was in my sixties and wondered if age had something to do with it. I was trying to think of everything that it could possibly be that was causing me to be so sick. In August of that year, I was about to fly to Houston to see my dad for my monthly visit with him. By this time, he was no longer in his home in Pasadena, Texas, he was in a memory care living home and was doing well. It was August, and I noticed that Hurricane Harvey was predicted to hit Houston with extreme force.

I waited two weeks after the hurricane had passed before I flew in to see him. The schedule I usually had was to fly in, rent a car, and check into my hotel that was across the highway from my dad's memory care home. I unpacked my suitcase and drove over to see my dad. I spent every day and evening with him for five days. Each night after dinner at the restaurant there, we went back to his room and watched *Wheel of Fortune*. I helped get him ready for bed, tucked him in, and said goodbye and I would see him tomorrow.

By this time, because of his Alzheimer's, my dad didn't recognize me. When I saw him, he would light up when I entered the room. I could tell that he knew that I belonged to him. I would always introduce myself as Jackie. After he was in bed, I gave him the sign of the cross with my finger on his forehead as he fumbled around to do the same with me. I kissed him, said I loved him and that I would see him tomorrow. I would leave the memory care unit for the night, get in

82

my rental car and drive to the hotel where I was staying. I grabbed something to snack on before bed and watched television to help me relax from the day.

I was watching the news that night in bed. They were talking about how everyone whose house flooded from the hurricane needed to rebuild very carefully. If they didn't rebuild correctly, paying close attention to dry everything out, issues from mold could arise. As they listed the health conditions that could arise from mold, I realized that I literally had every symptom that was listed. I immediately called my husband at the time. I told him what I had discovered.

I asked, "Do you think we have mold?" He comforted me and said we didn't have mold. However, I knew our basement flooded twice in the last fifteen years and perhaps we didn't dry it out properly. Again, he assured me that we didn't have mold. I didn't waver and made my beliefs known that it might be mold or something just as bad. I felt something inside of me telling me I was onto something and that I should continue to find out if our house was healthy or was it making me sick.

I knew it wasn't a coincidence that I happened to be in Houston after a hurricane and was watching the news that night. I began a necessary journey on finding out how I could be so sick on a constant basis. I felt like I should be healthier than I was. There was a knowingness deep inside of me that if I continued on this path of being sick, it would eventually take my life. I began doing deep research into finding a professional to inspect our home to see if they detected mold. I discovered that in addition to a visual inspection, they used specialized equipment to collect air and surface samples to send to a laboratory for analysis. I made an appointment for someone to inspect the house immediately.

The comprehensive report showed that our home had high levels of toxicity, so high that they would make a human incredibly sick, and the radon levels in our basement were at the maximum dangerous levels.

Finding that out, I began the journey of costly remediation to get rid of everything that made our house sick. I eventually put in a filtration system in our house, and within just a month, I began feeling healthy again. That experience taught me to not second guess myself. I was sitting in front of the television in Houston after Hurricane Harvey and I got the gift I was looking for, to find out what was making me so sick. I will be forever grateful for that news station and the timely events that occurred. However, I'm most grateful that I listened to that Inner Voice even though at the time it appeared to be buried inside me.

CHAPTER 8

I CHOOSE ME

Only think about the people you enjoy. Only read the
books you enjoy, that make you happy to be human. Only
go to the events that actually make you laugh or fall in
love. Only deal with the people who love you back, who
are winners, and want you to win too.
—JAMES ALTUCHER, *CHOOSE YOURSELF!:*
BE HAPPY, MAKE MILLIONS, LIVE THE DREAM

The last two years have been a transformative time in my life. I've
benefited from therapy at times throughout my life, but didn't have
a therapist for quite some time. In August 2022, my Inner Voice was
telling me I could use some guidance and tools to understand the
feelings and experiences I was going through. During my annual trip
to the retreat center in Tucson, I took a class on journaling and man-
aging stress from Michelle Fraley, MA, WPCC, a clinical counselor,

certified holistic coach, certified yoga instructor, meditation coach, and author of *Guided Journal for Self-Discovery and Balance: Reflections on All the Parts of You*.

I felt strongly that she would be the one to guide me through this transition I was struggling with. After class, I approached her and shared that I thought she might be a good fit for me as a therapist as I was going through a really difficult time. She requested that I email her. A couple of weeks later, I reached out to her to see if she received my email. She let me know that she was not currently seeing new clients, but at some point, she'd probably have an opening on her calendar. Two weeks later, I asked her if her schedule had opened up yet. She responded, "No, not yet, but I'll let you know when it does open up." A few weeks later, I emailed her again noting I was checking in and wanted to say hi and see if there were any openings available.

Each time I waited for her response, I would simply go about living my life. Then, when I thought about her again, I'd reach out to her. After contacting her several times, I received an email out of the blue. She let me know that she had an opening and asked if I wanted to take it. In that email, she shared that sometimes the squeaky wheel gets the attention. I guess I was the squeaky wheel! My persistence paid off. Even though she was in Tucson, Arizona, and I was in Minneapolis, Minnesota, the distance wouldn't be a hurdle whatsoever because now there was Zoom.

My Inner Voice let me know that Michelle was the right therapist for me. I needed someone to help me and take me by the hand and show me the way through this incredibly painful time. Working with Michelle was just what I needed.

During our sessions, we began working on something called a "2024 Game Plan." I decided I wanted joy and happiness in my life and to be with other people of like mind and energy. I wanted to be playful with others, laugh often, protect my peace, and focus on being healthy.

Creating a game plan feels empowering—it's like I'm an architect in charge of creating a masterful building. Consequently, I felt a whirlwind of emotions. After all, I was infused with this intense desire to create a better life and now I needed to gather the best tools to do so. Michelle Fraley helped me do that.

MY PATH TO CENTERING AND PEACE

I eventually found five things that I wanted to do each day to keep me centered, grounded, and peaceful. I looked for activities that would feed my body, mind, and spirit. If you'd like to try this, I suggest finding activities that work best for you and don't be afraid to switch it up if something is not working well for you. After all, you know yourself best.

The five things I chose were:

1. Do the Protection Rose meditation daily.
2. Do my physical therapy arm exercises daily.
3. Take my daily supplements.
4. Practice Qigong exercises daily.
5. Lay on my Spoonk mat bare backed for thirty minutes in the evening.

THE PROTECTION ROSE: A MINDFUL ENERGY BARRIER

I discovered the Protection Rose meditation from Janet Rae Orth while taking a class that focused on boundaries. The Protection Rose is a guided meditation that can protect you from other people's unwanted energy and make space for joy and vitality.

The technique can be helpful in many ways. Janet, the creator of the guided meditation I practice, suggests incorporating the visualization into daily routines. It can also be used before entering potentially challenging energetic situations. She recommends being consistent with the practice so it can develop into a habit.

It's a way for me to feel grounded daily and gives me a sense of peace. With time and dedication, the Protection Rose meditation has become a regular part of my self-care routine.

ARM EXERCISES

I do exercises on my rotator cuff daily to strengthen it so I can avoid rotator cuff surgery. I received the exercises from a trusted physical therapist at Twin Cities Orthopedics. I do the exercises because it is not only important to take care of my spirit and mind, but also my body.

DAILY QIGONG: HARMONIZE BODY AND MIND

I take a sixty-minute Qigong class twice a week. My instructor gave me a ten-minute video that I can use the other five days a week at home.

Qigong is an ancient Chinese practice that combines gentle movements, breathing techniques, and meditation. The benefits include both physical and mental well-being. Physically, it can improve flexibility, balance, and circulation, potentially lowering blood pressure and boosting your immunity.

DAILY SUPPLEMENTS: BRIDGING NUTRITIONAL GAPS FOR OPTIMAL WELLNESS

I take daily supplements from a homeopathic practitioner that uses muscle testing to find out what my body is lacking to fill any nutritional gaps in my diet and support my overall health and wellness.

THE SPOONK MAT: UNLOCK RELAXATION AND WELLNESS WITH EVERY PRICKLY POINT

The Spoonk mat has 6,210 acupressure stimulation points that, once pressed against troubled areas of the body, will increase circulation and relax stiff muscles and decrease pain. While lying on the mat, the body can release endorphins (pleasurable hormones), which induces a feeling of wellness and a positive attitude. Regular relaxation prevents the buildup of stress and manifestation of stress related diseases. When I used it the first time, I actually felt euphoric.

What I love about my Spoonk mat is that I can use it in ways that work for me. For example, you can use it for just five to ten minutes to energize yourself in the middle of the day. You can use it when you feel stressed or anxious and want to relax and recharge. Or you can use it to help you fall asleep. I'm committed to lying on it for thirty minutes every night before I go to bed. It helps put me in a relaxed state. I use a timer as I used to fall asleep on it. I even have a travel Spoonk mat that I take with me on trips so I can continue this practice no matter where I'm at.

My friend Mark tells me if you choose to do the same things that make you feel grounded each day for a week, you will feel like you're turning the needle. If you do these things for thirty days, you'll feel like you're on fire. Ninety days? Watch out, you're going to feel unstoppable!

But how to get into practicing these habits and getting on the path to feeling unstoppable? To find guidance I looked to James Clear, author of *Atomic Habits: An Easy & Proven Way to Build Good Habits & Break Bad Ones*. Clear says that every action you take is a vote for the type of person you wish to become and that "habit stacking" is one way to achieve this. I thought this could be the path for me and looked further into the practice of habit stacking. Clear explains that "you're more likely to stick with a habit when you pair it with an already existing habit like brushing your teeth, making the bed, taking a shower, or driving your car. We can piggyback onto other existing habits to create new habits. It takes all the thinking out of creating a new habit." I thought, *Taking small actions like these could definitely get me—and keep me—on my path to centering and peace!* Now, after I brush my teeth, I automatically sit down and practice the Rose Protection meditation. From there, I go right into doing my ten-minute Qigong before I start my day. After I eat lunch, that's my time to take my supplements.

BODY, MIND, AND SPIRIT

My five practices nourish my mind, body, and spirit. The Rose Protection meditation protects and strengthens my mind, Qigong cultivates and balances my spirit, vitamin supplements and physical therapy aid and nurture my body while the Spoonk mat nourishes all three to enhance my mind, body, and spirit. For me, if I focus too much on one aspect, I can feel off center. I need to bring the whole picture into balance. It's kind of like the weather. If you get too much sun, it brings the body off kilter a bit. The same applies to too much wind or rain. I need to balance myself to feel peaceful.

Besides the five things I do each day, I make an effort to incorporate other activities to bring joy into my life. I am eager to think about what lies on the horizon for me. To help clarify that, Michelle Fraley gave me an exercise where I journaled about what I was hopeful about.

I wrote:

- Warm weather
- Laughing a lot
- Wearing cute summer dresses
- Wearing sandals
- Walks by the lakes
- My freedom
- Travel
- Being with people who love me and want to be playful with me
- Good food
- Discovering a new fun side of me
- Peace inside; balance
- Going to new restaurants
- Enjoying my apartment in the spring, summer, and fall
- Publishing my new book and seeing it hit the bookstores
- Selling my condominium
- Abroad adventures
- Hanging with Tanner
- A New Beginning
- Being with people who are positive about life

- Life Itself
- The new experiences that are coming my way
- Professional speaking again on a new platform
- Jackie 2.0
- Living life with joy and a smile on my face
- Iced tea

It didn't take me long to create this list. By doing so, I could see I had a lot to look forward to. I truly felt empowered. In addition to looking forward to what the future holds, I practice positive self-talk to get me through rough days. For me, the most empowering way to do this is through "I AM" statements like:

- I am going to get through this.
- I am honoring and taking care of my energy.
- I am healthy.
- I am wealthy.
- I am safe and secure.
- I am happy.
- I am confident and proud of who I am.
- I am in charge of my own happiness.
- I am excited about all the possibilities.
- I am full of wisdom.
- I am in charge of my life.
- I am in alignment with my assignment.
- I am free.
- I am grounded and at ease.
- I am hopeful.
- I am courageous.

These "I AM" statements or affirmations empower me to focus on what I want rather than letting my mind run away with thoughts that may not be in my best interest. I like to read from Louise Hay's *Power Thought Cards*. I shuffle the card deck each day, pick a card, and read it. That's my affirmation thought for the day. Hay reminds me that "affirmations are like planting seeds in the ground. It takes some time to go from a seed to a full-grown plant. And so it is with affirmations—it takes some time from the first declaration to the final demonstration. So be patient."

In Richard Noel's book, *Creating Joy and Harmony, Volume 1,* he notes that each "I AM" statement should be followed by an enthusiastic "YES, I AM!" He believes the "I AM" consciousness is not something we turn on or off; it should become a habitual, repetitious standard operating procedure in our lives.

He advocates that life is short and we need to stop putting off things. I immediately took his message to heart. His workshop and book inspired me to think differently about my life. I am intentional about being the best me I can be, making sure that joy and laughter are a part of each day I strive daily to not take things for granted. I strive to live in the *now* instead of being stuck in the past or worrying about the future.

When my Inner Voice speaks up, I listen to it. If the message is to set up a doctor's appointment, I do it *now*. If I want to compliment somebody, I say it *now*. Be free and sincere with your compliments. If I am feeling love toward someone, I express it *now*. I don't hold back or wait until tomorrow. Tomorrow might never come. However, we are promised the here and now. Life is a privilege.

When anxious thoughts creep up while driving in my car, I gently guide my attention back to the present moment. I pause to ask myself, *What beauty am I overlooking right in front of me?* Perhaps its snowflakes drifting onto the glistening pavement, warm sunlight streaming through my window, or autumn trees painting the landscape in brilliant reds and golds.

Noel has so many phrases that encourage abundance and prosperity in our lives. Two of my favorites are, "Go where you feel happy, not where you feel crappy" and "Go where you feel adored, not where you feel ignored." At the time, that was something I needed to hear. From the first day I heard it, I knew this would be instrumental in moving me into the next phase of my life. And it has. Being dismissed, put down, or devalued are red flags that something is wrong. I know it's time to change the course of direction.

While it may not be life changing if it happens once, you don't want it to become a pattern. When you continually feel ignored, thrown under the bus, or criticized and don't do anything about it, it can keep happening. Before you know it, you wake up one morning, you look in the mirror, and you don't recognize yourself anymore. You can't believe you've put yourself in situations that weren't the best for you. This was my experience. When you feel ignored, it becomes problematic in every way—spiritual, mental, emotional, and physical.

NEVER GIVE YOUR POWER AWAY

Sarah Woodhouse recently wrote a blog post, "A Simple Guide to Owning Your Power" that spoke to me. According to her, true power comes from embracing your authentic self and living honestly. Each person's power is unique because everyone's authentic self is different.

For me, living authentically means embracing all aspects of yourself, including strengths and vulnerabilities. It means not hiding parts of yourself out of fear, speaking your truth, and avoiding self-judgment. Living authentically all begins with practicing self-acceptance, which requires hard work.

In today's world, comparing ourselves to others is common. Maybe we are jealous of others because they are cuter, younger, and thinner than us. Comparisons like these are not helpful; they are hurtful. We need to accept and start loving ourselves. It all starts here. Self-acceptance is doing good things for yourself, just like a good friend would want for you.

When you unconditionally love yourself, life becomes more manageable. As we get older, we have to unlearn many of the beliefs we've held onto since childhood to find that self-acceptance. By loving ourselves as we are, we can attain inner peace and happiness that can't be found anywhere else. We no longer have to attach ourselves to others for our happiness. Our power is not to be given away.

Woodhouse's blog reinforces my belief that we are much more powerful than we realize, and there's no better time than now to live a life rich in self-acceptance. That's how I choose to live my life moving forward.

CHAPTER 9

AWAKENING SELF-PRIORITY

Charting a New Course

Taking care of yourself isn't a luxury, it's a necessity.
—AUDREY LORDE

I know it's time to start putting my needs first instead of putting other people's needs first every time. I want to trust that good will come my way, instead of being afraid of life hurting me. I'm going to stand up for myself instead of being afraid of hurting the feelings of others.

I want to prioritize myself.

I choose to be with people that align with my values. However, I still have people in my life who don't align with my values and that's

okay. It's not my job to change others. It is my job to stand up for myself.

At age sixty-nine, I'm just starting to shape my life from this point forward. When I'm around people that don't align with my values, I can feel it inside. It's like a soft, tiny, little nudge that something doesn't feel right. Sometimes I can't put my finger on it, but I can feel it in my gut.

My hope is that this book will inspire you to look at your life through a different lens and learn to love all versions of yourself and know the best is yet to come. Note that what I'm sharing with you is my pathway to a better life for me. Your pathway may look very different. We all want different things out of life. Our core values influence what that pathway looks like. Typically, we learn those core values early on.

HOW CORE VALUES HELP US FIND OUR PATHWAY

Core values are our rules or guidelines for how we want to live our lives. They are the most important beliefs and principles that *really* matter to us. Core values shape how we behave and the choices we make.

Imagine our values as a compass that points us in the direction of how to act. If being kind is one of your core values, then your compass will lead you to make decisions and do things that show kindness to people.

Our core values make up your character—the qualities that define who we are as a person deep down inside. Our core values guide our goals, relationships, and how we spend our time.

We all have different values that are important to us. By knowing your core values, it becomes easier to stay true to yourself, instead of just going along with what others think you should do or value.

When our core values don't align with our actions, it can lead to feeling conflicted, guilty, or unsatisfied with ourselves. Our core values are kind of like an inner compass that helps guide us on the right path through life. When we don't act according to our values, it creates an uncomfortable feeling It's like there's a tug-of-war going on inside of us between what we did and what we really want to be true to.

But sometimes we might get distracted or make choices that go against what's important to us deep down. For example, if being honest is one of your core values, but you end up telling a lie, you'll probably feel guilty afterward. That's because your actions didn't match up with your value of honesty.

Living by our core values takes practice, but it's important because it helps us feel good about ourselves and at peace with our choices. When our actions match our core values, we'll feel more satisfied and truer to who we are.

I feel like I was born with my core values or acquired them at an early age. I probably learned some of them from my dad as we had similar values. I don't believe they've changed over the years. However, my appreciation and awareness for them have grown.

If I find myself around those that don't align with my core values, I make sure that my time is limited with them.

Throughout the years, I've learned how to stand up and appreciate my core values. In the past, I overrode or overlooked them. I come from a long line of family members that didn't speak up for themselves. Now I have clear boundaries when it comes to my core values. With age and experience comes confidence that allows me to speak up more and set boundaries. The only person who can fulfill us is ourselves, not others.

I was talking to Michelle Fraley about how disappointing it can be when someone lets you down. That's when she told me that it was time to fasten my seat belt and talk about the role of difficult people in our lives—they will inevitably let us down. She told me to accept and assume that difficult people are always going to be difficult. That difficulty may show up in different ways including being critical, late, controlling, or perhaps negative around every turn. Difficult people are never going to show up for others unless it benefits them or how they look to the people around them.

I keep fooling myself that my encounters with difficult people will be different. Michelle provided some great advice, "Once you know that the person is difficult, it's up to you how you choose to let that person in your life. You don't have the power to make someone less critical or less controlling."

We get evidence all the time about what people are like. I think Maya Angelou said it best, "When someone shows you who they are, believe them the first time." Right off the bat, they show you who they are—pay attention to that. I've had to let go of important relationships that I built my life around because they didn't align with my core values.

Here are some of my most important core values:

- Honesty
- Doing the next right thing
- Compassion
- Playfulness
- Empathy
- Being dependable
- Taking responsibility

- Integrity
- Trustworthiness
- Being a good friend
- Kindness
- Patience
- Respect
- Loyal
- Humility

As I continue on my transformation journey, I see someone emerging who is confident and knows her boundaries. Michelle Fraley likes to call her Jackie 2.0.

CHAPTER 10

MY JOURNEY TO JACKIE 2.0

I hope you find time tc be happy. Not just strong.
—LOUISE KAUFMANN

What really drew me to Michelle Fraley was her holistic approach and philosophy of helping people recognize that the best version of them already exists. When I was introduced to Michelle several years ago, little did I know that I would be creating a new version of myself, something that Michelle refers to as Jackie 2.0. Jackie 1.0 was the old version of myself. While Jackie 1.0 and 2.0 share the same core values, Jackie 2.0 is able to articulate them much more powerfully.

Michelle reminds me to never forget that Jackie 1.0 got me to where I am today. Jackie 1.0 was a capable woman so there's no need

to feel sad for her. She wasn't a wounded bird at all. That Jackie was okay. And here's why:

- Jackie 1.0 got me to a retreat center so I could begin healing.
- Jackie 1.0 showed up every step of the way for me.
- Jackie 1.0 mothered her son, made dinners, got her hair done, and wrote books.
- Jackie 1.0 never gave up on herself even when things were hard.

Thanks to my work with Michelle, I now know in my heart that Jackie 1.0 was a warrior despite everything she went through. I tell her, "Thank you for helping me learn all these lessons and giving me the strength to show up for myself."

I'm excited about the life I'm creating as Jackie 2.0, but I will never forget what Jackie 1.0 did for me. Jackie 1.0 was often on autopilot because she had so much to do. Whether I liked it or not, I would find myself at times feeling sad. There was so much to process while going through this transition that I didn't really see coming.

A SELF-COMPASSION SCRIPT THAT OFFERS COMFORT AND EMOTIONAL RELIEF

I'm so grateful I had Michelle Fraley by my side through this process. She shared a script with me to help comfort myself and others. It goes like this (fill in the blanks):

Right now, a part of me is feeling _____.

It can be challenging to be feeling _____.

I know I have felt _____ in the past and I know this feeling won't last forever.

While I am feeling _____, I will choose to be gentle and kind with myself.

By using this script, I've found labeling and expressing an emotion takes the discomfort or "punch" out of the emotion. When I practice self-compassion to calm my nervous system, it also calms my mind, body, and spirit.

MY DREAMS

At one point, I started to notice that my dreams were taking off and having a mind of their own. I didn't necessarily know what I dreamt when I woke up in the morning, but I knew I was having bad dreams, and I woke up feeling sad as a result. It typically took me at least thirty minutes to shake it off.

Michelle reminded me that as we dream, we tap into our subconscious. While we can't control what we dream about, we can offer ourselves grace.

What goes on in our dreams is our subconscious brain venting, processing, and making sense of things. I knew in my awake life that I was going through so many challenges, changes, and feelings all at the same time. Our brains get overworked all day, so it is important not to put any demands on our brains when sleeping.

It made sense that my subconscious brain found a way to let go by dreaming. I had to remind myself that it's okay. I'm safe. I had to stop getting upset with myself. Rather, I decided to give my subconscious the space it needed to do what it needed to do. I had to remind myself that what I'm going through—selling my home and furniture, moving to a different location, and letting go of an important relationship—are all difficult things to do.

Michelle asked me to think of it this way: During sleep the subconscious mind is clearing out the garbage that is holding us back; kind of like taking out the trash. The worst thing we can do is be mad at our brain for doing this.

Once I started to talk to my subconscious before I went to sleep, to let it know that I was holding space for it to do what it needed to do, my sleep became better.

THE ROLE OF SELF-EMPOWERMENT DURING MY JOURNEY OF PERSONAL TRANSFORMATION

During my transformation, I realized that I had put myself in situations where I didn't honor myself nor my feelings. I gave it to others that didn't give it back. I now realized I had done that for too many years. As I started incorporating the five things into my daily routine that kept me present and grounded, I knew I was being true to myself while honoring my feelings and who I am.

I began trusting my Inner Voice when it came to a "Hell No" and "Hell Yes." I started to let go of expectations and I didn't get drawn into the past. I knew every step I took was a step in the right direction. I started recognizing kindness in my everyday interactions. I'll let you in on a secret: kindness is everywhere! Maybe it's the server who is warming up your cup of coffee, somebody holding a door open for you, or a friend who takes time out of their schedule to drive you to the airport or a doctor's appointment.

Sometimes kindness has four legs and a tail.

A HORSE'S SIXTH SENSE

At the retreat center that I go to annually, they offer equine therapy. Equine therapy proves to be particularly helpful for people due to the unique nature of horses and their interactions with humans. Horses are highly sensitive and responsive animals, capable of mirroring human emotions and behaviors. This allows people to gain insight into their own emotional states and how they interact with others.

The physical presence and nonjudgmental nature of horses can create a sense of safety and calm, reducing anxiety and stress. Working with these large animals also builds confidence, as people learn to communicate effectively and establish trust with the horse. The hands-on, experiential nature of equine therapy can promote holistic healing.

This form of therapy can be especially beneficial for those dealing with trauma, anxiety, depression, and interpersonal difficulties. Horses have an innate ability to feel the emotions of humans. They recognize if you're real or if you're hiding something and not being true to yourself. During my first session with Eros, when he felt I wasn't aligned to my true self, he would walk away. I left that session knowing I had more work to do as he picked up on my senses.

I decided to book another one-on-one session with the instructor and Eros on my next trip in August 2024. Eros was off in the distance hanging out with other horses when I arrived. The instructor called for Eros and he came over. She shut the gate as we were in another fenced area. Eros had a cover over his eyes so the bugs wouldn't get in them. She took this off and I started petting him and touching his face. It was an incredible experience.

Evidently, I had some emotional stuff to let out. Sometimes when I feel sad, I tend to stuff it down just so I can feel happy instead of really letting go and feeling the feelings. And I know I really need to pick these feelings up instead of putting them down. I started to realize all the changes I made in my life in the past two years. It was a lot: I sold my home of over thirty years, got a divorce, let go of relationships that were important to me, and sold most of my possessions.

Our session was ninety minutes, but it felt like it went by so fast. As I was letting go of all those things, I could feel I had yet to truly cry out all my emotions about these events. That occurred to me as I put his face on my face. He put his head on my left shoulder, and I wrapped my arm around his face. I just stood there with him.

We were there for a long time with his head on my shoulder. Then, he moved positions so I could see his right side and touch his face. As I stood there looking at the front of his face, these emotions started to come out, and I started to cry. As I was crying on Eros, the instructor said, "Make sure you let Eros know that this isn't about him." So I said to the horse, "Eros, this is my stuff that's coming up. And I just need to let it out."

I started to cry on the side of his face, and then on the front of his face. He stood still as I continued to cry. It felt like I was crying on his face for about fifteen minutes. He then put his head back on my shoulder again. That's when the instructor asked me if I wanted to pick up his hoof as I had done that the previous year. I asked Eros if I could pick up his hoof, he lifted it up and I cradled it in my hand and let it down. Then, the instructor asked if I wanted to lift the front hoof. I did and as I was moving, for some reason, I started worrying about something and Eros literally just walked away from us.

I shouted, "Come back, Eros!" He came back. I told him I was going to pick up his hoof in the front. As I was about to pick up his hoof, he walked away again. And the instructor said, "What are you feeling right now?" And I said, "Well, I'm probably worrying about whether he's going to let me pick his hoof up." And that's when she said, "Just be in the moment." As soon as I started to think about something or worry about something or feel something else that wasn't in the moment, I let it go. During this process, Eros walked away several times, but he'd come back when we called him.

The next time he walked back, I was in the moment. I said, "Eros, I'm going to pick up your hoof." But I wasn't positioned right. I was asking the instructor where I should be positioned, and she didn't say much. I picked up the hoof which didn't come much off the ground. He put it down and I said, "Thank you. Eros."

A year prior during my first session with Eros I was afraid to walk behind him because I didn't want to get kicked. That first year I couldn't do it. The instructor asked me, "Well, what's the worst thing that can happen if you walk behind him?" I said, "He'll kick me." That's when we talked about the concept of fight or flight. I have a tendency to bring up the topic of fight and flight because of experiences like the hijacking where I learned to fight. If you continually wonder when something bad is going to happen again, you are continually on alert, which can cause a lot of stress on you when living like that. And I knew I didn't want to live like that anymore.

It came time to walk behind Eros. The instructor said, "Let's walk behind him together." She went first, and I went behind her. While I was touching him with both hands, she said, 'We're going to walk behind you, Eros." I followed her every step. We made our way around Eros, eventually touching him just behind his tail. Then, we did it again. It was now my turn to do it alone. I froze as I didn't have the courage at the time to go behind him by myself.

Then, I started talking more to my instructor. As we did, Eros walked away and then came back. As we continued talking, Eros positioned himself with his butt in front of me. The instructor said, "Look what he's done. He wants to give you another chance."

I told her I wanted to do it with her again. So, we did. Then, I knew it was time for me to go behind him alone. Since meeting Eros last year, I knew I could do it as I had built a year of confidence behind me. I told the instructor I was ready. I said, "Okay, Eros, I want to walk behind you." I touched him with both hands, and she instructed me to breathe as I walked behind them. But, as soon as I started to worry, he walked away. He just left me. I called him back. When he came back, he was right in front of me. The instructor asked me, "What are you feeling? Are you ready?"

I said, "Yes, I'm ready!" I then told Eros, "I'm going to walk behind you. It's important to me that I walk behind you and I'm going to let go of any worry." I took a deep breath, let go of any thoughts that came in my mind, and walked behind Eros by myself. He let me do it, and then I did it again. I couldn't believe I had done it. I had always heard that one should never walk behind a horse because of the danger of being kicked; it seemed I had internalized and clung to the danger and fear associated with this risk. Now I understood there could be a safe way to complete this task, which allowed me to release my deep-seated fear, conquer my self-doubt, and regain my confidence with Eros, and with my life. I'll never forget the emotional release I had with Eros as I cried on his face.

Personal growth has always been important to me and these experiences at the retreat center have allowed me to carve out time and see the importance of releasing emotions.

Releasing these emotions ties into letting go of attachment, and I had a lot to let go of, especially in the last two years. Some of the emotions I had released with the help of Eros were those attached to my house. Selling my house of thirty years because of my divorce made me realize how much we attach ourselves to our homes. I was heartbroken to lose it. It was kind of weird, but I felt like I was doing a disservice to the house by letting it go. I was attached to it. My counselor told me not to feel bad for the house and not to make the house something that it really wasn't.

We did an exercise where she was the house and I was Jackie and we had conversations while in these roles. Then, I was the house and she was Jackie. The exercise was super helpful as I didn't realize how much time and energy I put in my home to make it beautiful; I had gotten a lot of energy and sweetness from that house.

When it comes to attachment, we can learn from the Buddhists. In Buddhism, attachment is a primary cause of human suffering. It's defined as grasping or clinging to people, objects, ideas, or experiences, and it can bind people to impermanent things, leading to distress. There is a mistaken belief that possessions will bring us lasting happiness and fulfillment Attachment arises from our desire to feel secure, comfortable, and in control of our lives.

When we attach to people or things to try to make us happy or fulfilled, we get in trouble as the only person that can truly make us happy is ourselves.

It was time to let go of my attachments, and Eros with his sixth sense, his remarkable ability to sense and respond to human emotions and authenticity, helped me on this journey—my journey to Jackie 2.0.

EMBRACING JACKIE 2.0: A JOURNEY TO SELF-CONFIDENCE AND AUTHENTIC LIVING

As I continue to embrace Jackie 2.0, I make a firm stand that from this day forward, I get to decide who has the privilege to be in my life. They need to add value to it. I will ask myself, "Am I getting a good return on my emotional investment?"

If there's a pattern of feeling less than when I'm around them, then it's time to re-evaluate my relationships. Through Michelle, I've learned that our time is an investment. If I'm giving a friend my time, do I feel good or do I feel taken advantage of? If I choose to spend time with someone, I want us to focus on each other or I'm going to remove myself from the relationship.

Self-confidence is something I've explored in therapy. I told Michelle that I thought I had good self-confidence, but as we started to work together, I realized that my self-confidence needed some attention. She says, "There are sneaky ways that insecurities can creep in and can show up in our lives."

Here are some sneaky ways insecurities can show up in our lives:

1. Overthinking and Hesitating: I used to regularly ask others for their opinion and would even rely on friends to help make my decision. It could be something like asking a friend whether I should buy a red car or blue car or a black or yellow dress. Without really realizing it, I did it a lot. Michelle helped me realize that by asking and relying on other people's opinions, we are lowering our self-confidence.

2. Hiding: When we hide who we really are from others, we don't readily share our opinions, ideas, or dreams. That's both a disservice to us and others.

3. Complaining or Victim Mentality: With thinking like this, it's always everyone else's fault and we don't take responsibility for our actions.

4. Comparing: When we compare ourselves to others, it's easy to get trapped into thinking that everyone's life is better than ours. When we seek satisfaction from outside influences and possessions, we're bound to be disappointed.

5. Fear and Catastrophe: It's easy to get caught up in the gloom and doom when we are continually asking, "What if? What if I'm alone forever? What if the train I take goes off rails while I'm in it? What if I get the flu when I travel? What if I open myself to love and it doesn't work out?"

What Michelle shared with me was eye opening. I recognized that I often hesitated, hid, and compared myself to others. I also saw that I was busy people pleasing, worrying, and overthinking everything. These sneaking behaviors were impacting my self-confidence. I wasn't listening to my Inner Voice like I wanted to.

Michelle noted that we are all one-of-a-kind, special, and unique people based on our genetics and experience. She gave me some journaling homework which I'm happy to share with you.

In the first journaling prompt, I was asked to name three things that made me unique and special and wanted to know how they showed up for me. I wrote:

- I'm kind and love talking to everyone.
- I love giving compliments to others.
- I'm upbeat, love to learn, and am curious.

Next, she wanted to know what my biggest strengths and most prominent traits were. I wrote:

- I'm strong mentally, can get through hard times and come out smiling.

113

- I see the good in things.
- I love to connect with people.
- I pay attention to my Inner Voice.

Next, she wanted to know what my three top priorities at the time were. I wrote:

1. Check in with my son on a regular basis to say hi and let him know that I love him, have his back, and I'm very proud of him.
2. Take some time to decompress and go somewhere warm.
3. To downsize and let go of things I no longer need or want.

Next, I was asked to finish the following sentence: *I feel best about myself . . .*

1. When I do my Qigong practice every day.
2. When I speak up for myself.
3. When I'm outside in the sun.
4. When I'm careful who I choose to spend time with.
5. When I'm lighthearted, peaceful, and grounded.
6. When I keep good thoughts in my head.
7. When I spend my time wisely and not just haphazardly fill up my day.
8. When I laugh often.
9. When I'm in the zone, in tune to my Inner Voice.

Next, I answered the question, *When do you feel most confident?*

1. When I wake up
2. When I'm working on a project.
3. When I'm spending time with my son.

Next, I answered the question, *Who or what has a positive impact on my confidence?*

1. My son Tanner. He reminds me how much he loves me, how happy he is that I'm happy, he lets me know how much I mean to him.
2. My best friend Mark. He reminds me of the good I have in me.

During my next session with Michelle, we reviewed my homework. Then, she asked me, "What would you do if you had more confidence? How would you speak differently to yourself? What hobby would you try? What opportunities would you explore if you had more confidence?

Here is my list:

1. Go to Italy by myself.
2. Don't ask others for their opinions about what's best for me.
3. Spend time only with people who love me and want the best for me.
4. Let go of friendships that no longer serve me.

In less than two years, I've done all those things on that list. I've regained that lost confidence. I was on a mission to live life to the fullest while keeping my mind, body, and soul alive.

CHAPTER 11

KEEPING MIND, BODY, AND SPIRIT ALIVE

You have to leave the city of your comfort and go into
the wilderness of your intuition. You can't get there by
bus, only by hard work and risk and by not quite knowing
what you're doing, but what you'll discover will be wonderful. What you'll discover will be yourself.
—ALAN ALDA

I like that the mind, body, and spirit connection recognizes that human beings are complex, multidimensional entities where these three aspects are deeply intertwined and constantly influencing each other. When we neglect one aspect, it often leads to imbalances in the others. For instance, chronic stress (a mental state) can manifest as physical ailments like headaches or digestive issues, while also

dampening our spiritual well-being or sense of purpose. By nurturing this connection, we can create a powerful synergy that enhances overall well-being and quality of life.

By consciously cultivating the mind-body-spirit connection, we can achieve a more holistic state of health and happiness. This approach encourages us to address our physical health through proper nutrition and exercise, our mental health through practices like meditation and therapy, and our spiritual health through activities that give us a sense of meaning and connection to something greater than ourselves. When these three aspects are in harmony, we tend to feel more balanced, resilient, and fulfilled. This integrated approach to wellness can lead to improved physical health, greater emotional stability, enhanced creativity, better relationships, and a deeper sense of purpose and contentment in life.

HOLISTIC HARMONY: NURTURING THE MIND-BODY-SPIRIT CONNECTION IN CHALLENGING TIMES

I'm always seeking fresh perspectives on ways to incorporate and engage my mind, body, and spirit. According to Bonnie Mehr, director of the Dr. Diane Barton Complementary Medicine Program and director of integrative oncology at MD Anderson Cancer Center at Cooper University Health Care, the main concept behind the mind-body-spirit connection is pretty basic—

> We are all more than just our thoughts. We are also our bodies, our emotions, and our spirituality. All of these things combine to give us identity and determine our health and make us who we are.

Looking back, while we might have joked with our friends, family, and coworkers about the benefits of COVID-19 restrictions such as binge-watching Netflix or working from home in our pj's, the truth is, most of us felt some degree of stress and anxiety. If we didn't find constructive, healthy ways to cope, our bodies and minds eventually started showing signs that stress was taking its toll, whether we admitted it or not.

Mehr believes that people who exercise regularly, whether it's a daily walk, a long run, doing thirty burpees daily like my friend Mark does, an hour of yoga, or time in the gym strength training, often experience depression if their exercise routine is interrupted by injury, travel, or anything that prohibits them from getting the activity their body has come to expect and rely on for stress relief.

She also mentions the effects of being a stress eater on the mind-body-spirit connection. I know I have had that challenge myself when I was going through the hard transformation of change and challenge I found myself on.

Mehr says it's important to take time to pamper ourselves. I like getting a massage, getting my nails done, taking the time to have my hair cut, colored, and styled, taking walks, and enjoying a delicious meal, for example. I feel that by honoring myself, by acknowledging my body and the work it does for me in these ways, the mind-body-spirit connection is being fostered to make me feel good.

Finally, Mehr mentions the damage that long- and short-term stress can cause to our mind-body-spirit connection. But as I have learned from Mehr and from my own experiences of the physical, emotional, and mental trauma of the hijacking to the diagnosis, surgery, and healing from colon cancer—we need to pay attention to those stressors and not take for granted that our bodies will bounce back for us time and time again. Through being mindful of our stress level and taking action to counter it, we can foster our mind-body-spirit connection.

DIFFERENT OPTIONS FOR CREATING MIND-BODY-SPIRIT CONNECTION

- Journaling
- Laugh—watch a funny movie or go to a comedy show, for example
- Have the energy cleared in your home
- Reach out to old friends
- Volunteer at your favorite organization
- Try a new type of exercise that's out of your comfort zone
- Spend some time with animals, whether it be going to the zoo or petting a dog at the park or hanging out with your own pet
- Take time out of your day to enjoy a crafting class

THE MIND'S MEGAPHONE: HOW AFFIRMATIONS AND MANTRAS AMPLIFY PERSONAL EMPOWERMENT

Affirmations and mantras are powerful tools because they harness the incredible influence of our thoughts on our beliefs, emotions, and behaviors. By consistently repeating positive, empowering statements, we can gradually reshape our subconscious mind and override negative self-talk or limiting beliefs that may have been ingrained over time. Repetition helps to create new neural pathways in the brain, essentially rewiring our thought patterns to align with our desired self-image and goals.

The power of affirmations and mantras lies in their ability to shift our focus towards positive aspects of ourselves and our lives, boosting self-confidence and motivation. When we regularly affirm our strengths, capabilities, and worthiness, we're more likely to act in ways that reflect these beliefs, creating a self-fulfilling prophecy.

Besides that, mantras can serve as anchors during challenging times, providing a sense of calm and clarity. By centering our thoughts on empowering words or phrases, we can cultivate resilience, reduce stress, and maintain a more optimistic outlook. This positive mindset not only enhances our mental and emotional well-being but can also impact our physical health and the quality of our relationships, contributing to overall personal growth and success.

The following are some affirmations and mantras that have helped me get through my biggest life transition. I told myself:

- I don't have to have it all figured out right now to feel at ease.
- I trust myself and I trust the process.
- I'm going to be okay.
- I let go and let God take over.
- I take one day at a time.
- I'm leaning into self-trust.
- I love you, I love you. I love you, Jackie.
- I am happy to go through this journey.
- There's more in this world that I want to experience.
- Thank you for being on my side.
- I look forward to this year.
- I am beautiful.
- I am valued in this world.

- I can get through this.
- I love and enjoy my newfound friends; we laugh, learn, and grow together.
- I believe that I can have a life that is truly joyful.
- I trust my body with loving kindness.
- I am calm, peaceful, and at ease.
- I am resilient.
- I am in charge of my own happiness.
- If I'm not making mistakes, I'm not making much of anything.
- This is tough, but I'm tougher.
- My life is full of possibilities.
- This is a simple challenge; my mind, body, and spirit are ready for this challenge.
- I smile and laugh a lot.
- I'm leaning in to make powerful changes.
- I'm somebody that cares about taking care of myself.
- I'm so proud of the person I am and the person I'm working to become.
- Whatever my plan is, I can make it happen.
- I am wise.
- I am lovable.
- I enjoy this life I have created for myself.
- I matter and I show myself that I matter.
- All is well in my world.
- Everything is working out for my highest good.
- Out of this situation, only good comes.
- I am safe.
- I let go of all expectations.

- I flow freely and lovingly with life.
- I believe that only good awaits me at every turn.

While these thoughts didn't remove suffering, it did something even more powerful. It removed me from being an active participant in my suffering. I started looking at things to align with what is the best version of me. The best version of me is kind, helpful, loving, generous, grateful, and energetic.

When you think about it, humans are social animals. We're all wired for connection. The more we can build positive relationships and develop cooperative connections, the more enriching our lives may be.

FINDING OUR PERSONAL MEANING

Discovering personal meaning is a profound and often lifelong journey of self-exploration and reflection. It involves delving deep into one's values, passions, and experiences to uncover what truly matters and brings fulfillment. This process often requires us to question societal expectations and our own ingrained beliefs, pushing us to look beyond surface-level satisfactions to find what genuinely resonates with our core selves.

Personal meaning can be found in relationships, career, creative pursuits, spiritual practices, or service to others. It's unique to everyone and may evolve over time as we grow and encounter new experiences. The quest for meaning often involves facing challenges and uncertainties, but it can lead to a profound sense of purpose, authenticity, and inner peace.

When we align our actions and choices with our personal sense of meaning, we tend to experience greater satisfaction, resilience in the face of difficulties, and a deeper connection to ourselves and the world around us. Ultimately, discovering personal meaning is about creating a life that feels true to who we are at our deepest level, and using that understanding to guide our decisions and shape our path forward.

As I delved into my own personal meaning, I had to ask myself, "What parts of myself have I neglected or put off that could have helped me on my journey?"

My answer forced me to confront some issues that were incredibly painful.

- I neglected the part of Jackie who loves to smile and laugh a lot.
- I ignored some Inner Voice messages that I needed to hear all in the name of making a marriage work.
- I put off making my marriage work with myself.
- I put off making decisions that have my best interest at heart; instead, I was trying to make someone love me.
- I put off being a good role model for my son and a good role model for myself.
- I stopped taking walks and being with nature to feed my soul.

As I continued to work with Michelle, she shared seven tips to help me level up which I found very helpful. They included:

1. **Be flexible and intuitive with plans and opportunities.** Say yes as often as possible with opportunities that your spirit believes is energy uplifting. Say no to opportunities

that suck your energy and spirit. Create balance between energy giving and energy sucking. Don't say yes to skipping something that uplifts you because there's not much time left in the day.

2. **Create and cultivate patience with yourself and others.** Do everything you can to be patient with healing through any transition. That includes the dreams you have while you're sleeping, patience when in traffic, and tolerance with your health. Being patient starts with your peace of mind.

3. **Welcome opportunities to step out of your comfort zone.** This might include activities like eating out by yourself at a restaurant, going on a vacation by yourself, or signing up for a group activity for the first time. Celebrate and congratulate yourself when you take any initiative to go outside your comfort zone.

4. **Love and honor yourself unconditionally.** That means loving and honoring yourself *now*, not when it's convenient.

5. **Give what you can everywhere you go.** Giving a smile, a sincere compliment, or someone your undivided attention can make an impact just as much as a financial donation.

6. **Speak positively about yourself and others as much as possible.** Be careful with your words; not just your words with others, but to yourself. It's time to let go of gossip, complaining, and the victim mentality.

7. **Choose to focus on what's working for you instead of what isn't.** This kind of thinking can promote a positive mindset.

ELEVATE YOUR FREQUENCY: A GUIDE TO
HARNESSING THE POWER OF HUMAN VIBRATIONS

Human vibrations refer to the idea that everybody emits a unique energetic frequency or "vibrational signature." This concept is rooted in the scientific understanding that all matter, including the human body, is composed of atoms in constant motion, creating energy fields.

Proponents suggest that our thoughts, emotions, and overall state of being influence these vibrations, with positive states like joy, gratitude, and love associated with higher frequencies, while negative states like fear, anger, or depression correspond to lower frequencies.

The idea of human vibrations extends to the belief that we can consciously alter our vibrational state through practices such as meditation, mindfulness, positive affirmations, and energy healing techniques. By raising our vibrational frequency, it's believed we can improve our physical health, emotional well-being, and even attract more positive experiences and relationships into our lives.

Penney Peirce, author of *Frequency: The Power of Personal Vibration*, explains how we have a personal vibration that radiates from us and how it changes depending on what we're thinking, feeling, and doing. She explains, "We're not only affected by our own vibrations, but also from the vibrations of everything around us which includes people, places, and things. Since everything is energy, it makes sense that all vibrations have an effect on us, both positively and negatively. The more we allow our souls to shine through us, the higher our personal vibration will be. The good news is that we can decide the frequency we want to live in because we have the power to influence our own personal vibration. Why do we want to raise our vibrational frequency? Because our lives expand when we're living at a higher vibrational frequency."

After reading this, I experimented with ways to raise my vibrational frequency. I discovered that raising my vibrational frequency was easier than I thought. It had a lot to do with mindset and being intentional. It could be simple things like watching an uplifting movie or looking at the world from a glass-half-full rather than a glass-half-empty perspective. It can be taking an impromptu walk and noticing nature's beauty. I make a concerted effort to look at the good instead of the negative. When my vibrational frequency increases, I feel a sense of happiness and peace in my body that resonates with my relationships, health, career, and finances.

Peirce outlines specific ways to raise our vibrational frequency noting we are all unique. For some, it's being authentic and keeping promises. For others, it might be giving something and expecting nothing in return like making an anonymous donation. Journaling can be incredibly helpful in raising your vibrational frequency too.

HOW JOURNALING CAN HELP WITH MINDFULNESS

Writing down our thoughts and feelings gives us a physical way to express and analyze our inner world, allowing us to better understand and grow from our experiences. Research suggests journaling can aid in emotional regulation and stress reduction, leading to better health. Here's an overview of some of the benefits:

1. **Stress reduction:** Writing about your thoughts and feelings can help release pent-up emotions and reduce stress.
2. **Self-reflection and insight:** Journaling provides a space for self-discovery and understanding your thoughts and behaviors better.
3. **Goal setting and tracking:** It's an effective tool for setting, planning, and monitoring progress towards personal goals.

4. **Improved emotional intelligence:** Regular journaling can enhance your ability to recognize and manage your emotions.

5. **Problem-solving:** Writing about challenges can help you gain new perspectives and find solutions.

6. **Creativity boost:** Free writing can unlock creativity and inspire new ideas.

7. **Memory enhancement:** Regularly recording experiences can improve memory retention and recall.

8. **Mood improvement:** Expressive writing can help alleviate symptoms of anxiety and depression.

9. **Conflict resolution:** Journaling about interpersonal conflicts can lead to better understanding and resolution.

10. **Improved communication skills:** Regular writing practice can enhance your overall communication abilities.

11. **Mindfulness practice:** Journaling can serve as a form of mindfulness, keeping you present and aware.

12. **Physical health benefits:** Some studies suggest journaling can boost immune function and speed up healing.

13. **Personal growth tracking:** A journal serves as a record of your personal development over time.

14. **Increased self-confidence:** Recognizing your progress and achievements through journaling can boost self-esteem.

15. **Gratitude cultivation:** Using a journal to regularly express gratitude can increase overall life satisfaction.

Journaling is a flexible and personalized practice that can be tailored to our individual needs and preferences, making it a valuable tool for personal development and well-being. We live in a world with never-ending distractions; journaling is a great way to break through the noise and check in with ourselves. It can help us understand our priorities and give our thoughts and feelings some structure and organization.

The following are different forms of journaling and journaling prompts given to me by Michelle Fraley along with my responses.

GRATITUDE JOURNALING: A reflective practice that involves regularly writing down things, experiences, or people you're thankful for in your life. This intentional focus on positive aspects of one's life, no matter how small, helps shift attention away from negative thoughts and cultivates a more appreciative mindset.

Some people dedicate a few minutes each day or week to jot down several items they're grateful for, which can range from significant life events to simple pleasures like a warm cup of coffee or a beautiful sunset. The power of gratitude journaling lies not just in the act of writing, but in the mental shift it promotes—encouraging people to actively seek out and acknowledge the good in their lives. This practice has been scientifically linked to numerous benefits, including increased happiness, improved sleep, reduced stress, enhanced empathy, and better overall mental and physical health.

What are three things I'm grateful for today?

I wrote:

- I am grateful for the beautiful flowers I see outside.
- The delicious pizza I had for lunch today.
- Writing this book and how grateful I am that I took that typewriting class in high school.

What are the three things that are working for me today?

I wrote:

- I had lunch with my son Tanner.
- I did my five things today to keep me grounded.

- I feel joyful and happy.

BULLET JOURNALING: Combines elements of a planner, diary, and to-do lists. At its core, it uses a series of simple symbols, or bullets, to quickly categorize and organize information, tasks, and events. Bullet journaling is flexible, allowing users to track habits, set goals, plan projects, and reflect on experiences all in one place. I like it to group together related ideas that spark joy, inspiration, and excitement for me.

What five movies can I watch over and over?
- Any movie with Ryan Reynolds and Jason Statham
- Date Night
- Last Holiday with Queen Latifah
- Migration
- Arthur the King with Mark Wahlberg

What five foods or snacks do I love to eat?

- Caesar salad with salmon
- Chilean sea bass
- Sweet, savory, and tart Trader Joe's Trek Mix
- Kettle corn
- A great cheeseburger with fries and ranch dressing

Who are six people I love spending time with?
- Joan Joyce
- My son Tanner
- Mark LeBlanc
- My great-nephews Marshall and Owen

- My nephew Michael Nirk

What are the five things I'm good at?
- Being a good friend
- Keeping in touch with those I love
- Decorating my house
- Coming up with ideas
- Being kind

AFFIRMATION/INTENTION JOURNALING: A powerful self-improvement practice that combines the benefits of positive affirmations with the reflective nature of journaling. The idea is to regularly write down positive, empowering statements about ourselves, our abilities, and our goals. The goal is to reinforce positive self-talk, challenge limiting beliefs, boost self-confidence, and align our mindset with our aspirations. Over time, this practice can help reshape thought patterns, enhance motivation, and foster a more positive outlook on life.

Writing down affirmations and forming intentions is all about creating a framework for how you would like to think, feel, or behave. You can practice writing your own affirmations using these prompts:

I am _____
I love _____
I choose _____
I release _____

My answers:

I am *at peace.*
I love *the beauty in nature.*
I choose *to live.*
I release *all my hurts.*

STREAM OF CONSCIOUSNESS JOURNALING: A free-flowing, unstructured writing technique that captures the continuous flow of thoughts, feelings, and sensations as they occur in the mind, without censorship or concern for grammar, punctuation, or coherence. This approach encourages people to put pen to paper (or fingers to keyboard) and write continuously for a set period, typically ten to thirty minutes, without pausing to edit, judge, or organize their thoughts. You can even start by writing freely for two minutes on any words, ideas, or thoughts that go through your mind without censoring your thoughts.

By doing so, you bypass the conscious, critical mind and tap into the subconscious, allowing for raw, authentic self-expression. This method can reveal hidden thoughts, fears, desires, and creative ideas that might not surface during more structured writing. It's often used as a tool for self-discovery, stress relief, problem-solving, and creative inspiration. Practitioners might find themselves jumping from topic to topic, exploring memories, processing emotions, or even writing nonsensical phrases as they maintain the continuous flow. The lack of rules and structure in stream-of-consciousness journaling makes it particularly effective for overcoming writer's block, exploring complex emotions, and gaining deeper insights into one's psyche.

PROMPTED JOURNALING: A structured approach to reflective writing that uses specific questions, themes, or prompts to guide the journaling process. Unlike free-form journaling, where writers might struggle with what to write about, prompted journaling provides a starting point or direction for exploration. This method is particularly helpful for those new to journaling or those who find a blank page intimidating.

What do you love to do?

I love trying new things and eating new foods.

What does your gut tell you that you were made to do?

To live the heck out of Life.

Finish this sentence: I feel best about myself when _____.

I feel best about myself when I'm laughing, being with friends who love me and want to be playful with me, and when I follow my bliss.

What do you need to let go of in order to move forward?

To let go of the notion that others know what's better for me, to let go of thinking that being with someone who is mean to me is better than being alone, to let go of thinking that change is hard and learn to flow with the flow of life and trust it to take me to a better place or situation than the one I'm in.

I never thought I would be one to journal as sometimes it's not easy for me to sit and write about my feelings, I'd much rather talk about them. But since I've been working with Michelle, I have started to buy into the idea that it gives me a window into my values, what's important and what's not important, and I answer questions about things I never gave much thought about. It also gives me an opportunity to create a life of intention and live an authentic life.

For this, I am grateful.

CHAPTER 12

EMBRACING A FRESH PERSPECTIVE

Someday, we'll look back and smile
And know it was worth every mile
—CHRIS STAPLETON, "STARTING OVER"

Songwriter and singer Chris Stapleton's song "Starting Over" is all about starting fresh, moving on, and finding hope in the midst of life's changes. I know from personal experience that starting over is never easy. In fact, it can be extremely painful and takes a lot of tenacity and willingness to make positive changes. A great way to start fresh is to make a plan for doing so. Michelle Fraley is big on choosing an assignment for the day, her term for making a plan, and aligning with it.

Choosing your assignment means deciding what deserves your energy and attention for the day when you wake up. By doing so, you're letting *you* decide what your assignment is—if you don't choose your assignment, someone will choose or give you your assignment or your intention for you.

Perhaps your assignment for the day is showing up for a friend at lunch, spending time with your child, spending quality time with your partner, to feel grateful today, to honor your body by eating healthy foods, walking, being creative, being playful, finding reasons to laugh, spreading kindness, uplifting yourself and others, to get out of the house and connect with people, to be generous and make a donation, or connect with God or your Higher Power.

Perhaps your assignment includes self-care for the day. That will look different for all of us. Perhaps it is getting a haircut, going to the doctor to check on something that doesn't quite feel right, going grocery shopping, watching a funny movie, getting a massage, working out, finding time to make a delicious nutritious meal, or relaxing in a comfortable chair.

If you are spending time worrying about the future, then you are not in alignment with your assignment.

IT'S TIME TO LOOK AT WHAT YOU WANT IN YOUR LIFE

To get an idea of what matters to you, ask yourself:

- What do you want to feel and experience more of today?
- What matters most to you?
- What do you need more of today?
- What do you need less of?

Ideally, we want to keep our power, protect our peace, and not give it away. Even if you have given your power away all your life, you can use today as the fork in the road, to choose to align with your assignment, to align with the values you choose, to align with the integrity you want to have, and to protect your peace.

Michelle Fraley said to think about it like this: You wouldn't let just anyone into your house to sleep in your bed or rummage through your refrigerator and eat your food, right? If that is how we feel, then why aren't we protecting our peace the way we protect our home?

When we feel empowered, we stop relying on other people to decide how we are going to think, feel, and act, including what we eat and what we wear. If it helps, think about yourself as a fussy consumer when it comes to your time and energy. Preserving it is a way to protect your peace.

We can go deeper by asking ourselves more questions like:

- What are we listening to? Is there criticism and complaining and negativity that we're hearing on a constant basis?
- What songs are we listening to?
- What are the things that we are looking at? Is it constant pictures of negativity?
- Are we hearing negative comments from a loved one, television, or our phone?
- How much time do we spend talking instead of listening?
- How much time are we giving to our phones instead of spending time with the people we love or being outside with nature?

Our thoughts create our reality. If we go in thinking something is going to be peaceful, we're going to find peace in it. If we think our situation is going to be like a dumpster fire, then we're going to see the negativity in it.

10 PRACTICAL STEPS TO PROTECT YOUR INNER PEACE

Keeping our peace and focusing on finding that peace in things that are challenging isn't always as easy as it may sound. There are things we can do that will help with that. Some practical things that we can do to protect our peace include:

1. Take care of yourself from the inside out
2. Manage your stress
3. Keep yourself flexible
4. Stay hydrated
5. Nourish your body with healthy foods
6. Connect with people who make you feel good, who supplement your peace
7. Limit interactions with people who detract from your peace
8. Show up with gratitude
9. Practice self-talk, prayer, mantras
10. Manage your expectations

WE ALL HAVE OUR OWN IDEAS ON WHAT FUELS OUR INNER PEACE

In an episode of Bria Gadd's podcast *The Period Whisperer*, she talks about the concept of *destination happiness*, the idea that we'll be happy in the future when we achieve a goal we've set for ourselves. Some of her examples of destination happiness are, "I'll be happy when the weather clears up," "I'll be happy when the kids go back to school," "I'll be happy when I lose twenty pounds," or "I'll be happy when everyone around me stops relying on me so much and helps me around the house."

What Gadd recommends countering our tendency to fall into thoughts of destination happiness is to find micro-joys. She describes micro-joys as "micro-moments of positivity, glimmers, moments in your day that make you feel shiny, that light you up." Her words made me remember to focus on what I have instead of what I don't have. Gadd challenges listeners to keep their eyes on their own paper. She encourages them to stop looking at what other people are doing and thinking and instead do what's best for them. By keeping my eyes on my own paper, my own life, I get to choose what is right for me.

When I heard Gadd's approach for shifting such an ingrained mindset as destination happiness, I jumped on it. I grabbed a pen and paper and listed out some micro-joys that I could celebrate. I scribbled:

- Going to see the magical lights on homes during Christmas
- How you look in the cute dress you bought
- The great cup of coffee you just drank
- The flowers and trees as they bloom in the spring
- The new friendship you found
- Soft pajamas
- Being a mom to my son
- Watching a good Hallmark movie
- Taking my bra off at the end of the day
- Baseball and football games
- Going to the movie theater

- Weddings
- A seafood dinner
- Going to a swimming pool
- A hot cup of tea at night
- Travel
- Qigong
- My beautiful apartment
- The fountain outside my door
- As the sun goes down before it gets dark
- Being around my nephews Marshall and Owen
- Mexican food
- The smell of Christmas time
- Walking on grass with my bare feet
- Listening to uplifting music
- Practicing yoga

I've heard and believe that people who show up and notice the little joys every day are the happiest people, fueling their inner peace by celebrating their micro-joys. I'm grateful I've found this tool for changing my own mindset, tapping into my inner peace, and raising my vibration.

WHEN LIFE DOESN'T GO AS PLANNED: FINDING YOUR 'TUSCAN SUN' MOMENT

In the 2003 movie *Under the Tuscan Sun*, Frances, portrayed by Diane Lane, goes through a very difficult divorce and is forced to sell her house. While on a tour of Italy, she makes a spontaneous and surprising choice to buy a villa in the Tuscany region of Italy. There is an interesting cast of characters that help her along the way. That includes a realtor that guides her through the process of buying a villa and lends a helping hand. She hires a crew to help her remodel and make the villa her own. Katherine, a blond-haired woman, is a constant throughout the movie giving her advice and telling her to stop being so sad. At one point, Katherine becomes frustrated with Frances feeling sorry for herself. She told her to go to her villa and focus on her home and live her life.

As Frances becomes stronger, she tells the realtor that all she wants in her Tuscany home is a wedding, a family, and laughter. On the day that a young couple gets married at her house, the realtor sat by Frances and reminded her that she got everything she wanted. She wanted a wedding at her home, and that's what happened with the young couple. She wanted a family, and that's what happened when her best friend and baby came to live with her, and she got laughter as she listened to the wedding party behind her laughing and having a good time. When the realtor pointed out to her that she got everything she wanted, she smiled.

When I found myself in the middle of letting go of a twenty-nine-year marriage that was important to me, I thought about *Under the Tuscan Sun* and used the advice of Katherine—to focus on my home and live my life. I began to fix up my apartment, to work on this book, spend time with people I trusted, and do the hard work on healing my hurts. I focused on building up my house within myself and outside of myself and all along continued to live my life.

In my own Tuscan Sun story, there were people like Mark LeBlanc, Michelle Fraley, Tanner Olsen, Anne Muree, Tejpal, Birgit Kraus, Laurie Wondra, Richard Noel, Rae Jessie Gordon, Emilia Cajigas, Lolita Leal, and many others who helped me along the way, encouraged me, and gave me advice.

Before I was even separated from my husband or divorced, I wanted a life that was truly joyful where people could truly love me and be playful with me. I wanted to speak up for myself and trust that that would not hurt anyone.

My separation and divorce happened despite what I wanted. That's okay. As the old saying goes, "You don't always get what you want, but you get what you need." Eventually, as I began healing from my divorce, I wanted a life that was truly joyful where people could truly love me and be playful with me and that's what I got.

I encourage you to focus on what you want and go and live your life and make choices that support what you want. Mark LeBlanc talks about adding little adventures to your daily calendar. Here are some of mine:

- Going to a new coffee shop
- Taking a leisurely walk around the neighborhood or lake
- Visiting a friend
- Visiting a museum
- Going to an outdoor festival
- Driving through a beautiful part of town where you live
- Going to an arboretum to see beautiful plants and flowers
- Buying flowers for yourself
- Going out for a hamburger with a friend
- Going to a local library to find a good book and sitting in a comfortable chair reading it
- Hanging out with a pet like a dog or cat
- Simply slowing down
- Visiting a restaurant you've been wanting to go to
- Enjoying a classic car show

- Taking a long bath surrounded by glowing candles
- Dancing (whether it's at home or out in public)
- Enjoying a picnic in the park
- Sitting by a bonfire in your backyard holding someone's hand

These are all just suggestions that can lighten us up, put a spring in our step, and a spirit in our voice. I know this to be true in my life. If I go more than two days without doing my Qigong practice, making a connection with someone, or getting outdoors, I begin to feel like things are closing in on me, and I begin to feel uneasy and nervous. Fitting one little experience a day in our very busy lives will help us to keep our joy and peace.

I'm a big believer in doing something for others and doing it daily. Whether it's holding a door open for someone, mowing a friend's lawn that needs help, shoveling snow off a neighbor's drive-way, making a meal to share, reading a book to someone who feels lonely, giving compliments to others, dropping off a birthday card in the mail to a friend or loved one, surprising someone with a gift, calling a friend out of the blue that you've been thinking about, or being kind to those around us. Doing something for others helps put a light-heartedness in our spirits.

SAVING OURSELVES

Recently, I watched the Netflix series *Nobody Wants This* starring Kristen Bell and Adam Brody. Adam's character, a rabbi, gives a sermon in a Jewish temple. He tells a story about a man who was stranded on the roof during a flood. The man questions God as to why He didn't come for him and save his life. Adam's character goes on to say, "God responded, 'I sent you a life jacket, a boat, and a helicopter. That was me, buddy.' We all have these chances to wake up and change the course of our lives. Everything can have purpose if we allow it. If you are thinking about switching careers, maybe that's God talking to you. If you are hesitating about making a big decision, that could be God telling you to think twice. But if you think God's plan is supposed to feel like something specific, and you haven't felt it, and you wonder if we're all in on some big secret that you're not in on, let me tell you, you're in on it, and that's it."

This scene spoke to me. The sermon simplifies the whole idea of listening to the whisper inside of us and our inner voice. If I had heard this advice early on in my life, I think it would have helped me recognize some of the thoughts and feelings that were coming through me that I was dismissing. Hearing this advice now allows me to listen to my Inner Voice even more closely.

EMBRACING ALL THAT LIFE HAS TO OFFER

I'll be turning seventy when this book is published. Michelle Fraley tells a story about having dinner with her dad, mother-in-law, and father-in-law who were all in their seventies. She asked them what their favorite decade was. Expecting they would choose a time when they were in their twenties or thirties; she was surprised when they told her the best decade was being in their seventies despite any health issues and challenges. Why? They shared how they have been experiencing freedom, wisdom, financial security, and a deeper sense of what matters to them. They no longer worry about other people's opinions.

After she shared this with me, I totally understood what they were saying. As I'm leaving my sixties, my sixties have been my favorite decade. In my sixties, I have evolved to feeling more at peace, centered, happy, and aligned with my values than I've ever been before.

IT'S ABOUT THE JOURNEY, NOT THE DESTINATION

In May 2017, I had an opportunity to stay on the island of Maui in Hawaii. I had heard about the Road to Hana for many years but wasn't quite sure what to expect. I joined a group and for some reason, we took our sweet time before leaving for Hana. Over lunch, we discovered by reading a brochure that it's best to start early.

Eventually, we piled into our white Jeep rental and off we went. I had money in my purse for when we went shopping at the cute shops once we arrived. I thought I was going to go shopping for a cute dress from Hana or a trinket to take home as a souvenir. Even though we were about to set off, I still knew so little—I wondered what the road to Hana was like and was Hana a town or a region?

From the brochure I learned that Hana is a town. We left Kahului in the county of Maui and traveled seven hours round trip to reach Hana, which is on the northern shore of Maui. The road is one lane on both sides and it's over and through the mountains. In some places, we had to share the road with drivers coming toward us, each taking turns. I was in the passenger seat, so I was able to take in the beauty. There are about 620 curves and 59 bridges and countless waterfalls.

The terrain and landscape were beyond words. Our driver had to be entirely focused on the road so as not to make a mistake. I was enamored by the stunning beauty of this rainforest, feeling like I was inside a piece of heaven.

As we finally made it to Hana, I didn't see any cute shops or restaurants. In fact, it looked more like a neighborhood. As we turned around to make the trip back to our hotel in Maui, I realized that the road to Hana was never about reaching Hana, it was all about the road itself and its surroundings.

It was like the old saying, "It's not about the destination, it's about the journey." The road to Hana has its twists, turns, potholes, speed bumps, and fender benders. And just like life, we have our twists and turns, challenges, heartaches, breakups, health issues, disappointments, and countless number of surprises that come our way throughout our lives, and we wonder, *How am I going to get through this?* But, if you stay with it, stay on the road of life, and lean on the angels that appear on your path to help out, the clouds clear, the storm passes, and the sun keeps shining.

ACKNOWLEDGEMENTS

This book was made possible by many people's generous support and hard work.

I want to thank Corrine Casanova, my editor, who worked diligently with me while writing this book. Your ability to put the puzzle pieces of this book together to make sense amazes me. You believed in this book from the beginning. I appreciate your patience, encouragement, and kind words throughout this project. My book came alive because of you. For that, I am incredibly grateful.

A special acknowledgement to Mark LeBlanc, who has been a guiding force in my life and a constant friend by my side. You believed in this book when I wasn't sure this was even a book.

Thanks to my publisher Soul Speak Press, for bringing my manuscript into book form. Jess Buchanan, Loren Buchanan, and Ilsa Manning, I've enjoyed our publishing journey together.

I have never-ending gratitude to Michelle Fraley. I appreciate you giving your permission for me to share our work together with the readers. Without your ideas, suggestions, and guidance, I would not be where I am today. I know that for sure. You helped me see the

light at the end of the tunnel. You showed me ways to come out of grief with hope and joy in my heart. I loved how our weekly Zoom sessions always began with you being so happy to see me. Jackie 2.0 would not have been possible without you by my side.

Others who have supported me and deserve recognition are Laurie Wondra, Dr. Michael Isaacson, Diane Rother, Anne Muree, and Birgit Kraus.

And finally, to my son Tanner, our weekly dinners put a smile on my face and a spring in my step. You make me laugh, and I love that you are my biggest fan. Your unconditional love uplifts me every day.

TO CONNECT WITH JACKIE OR TO LEARN MORE
ABOUT HER WORK, VISIT HER HERE:

www.ingramcontent.com/pod-product-compliance
Lightning Source LLC
Chambersburg PA
CBHW020355130626
46549CB00006B/2293